Our Victorious Lord Reigns Forever

Revelation 21:1—22:21

S0-CCA-180

Through seven sets of visions God has shown John, and us, "what must soon take place" (Revelation 1:1). He has taken us from Christ's ascension into heaven through the "last days," showing us both the trials that await His people and the judgment which He will visit upon the world because of human sinfulness. He has shown us that the events of history are in fact scenes of a cosmic battle between the forces of God and the forces of evil, and that Satan and his hosts will in the end be defeated and destroyed by God's direct intervention.

These things are told us to admonish us to remain faithful, but also to give us comfort in the face of the trials that will come, so that we may be assured that God's final triumph is certain. Each series of visions has looked at the end times from a slightly different standpoint than the previous ones; each has told us a bit more about God's purposes in human history.

1. New Heaven, New Earth, New Jerusalem (21:1–8)

After seeing the present age come to an end, John is shown a new heaven and a new earth. What is the nature of this new heaven and earth? Does it have any connection at all with the old? Peter's description of the destruction of the old, "The heavens will disappear with a roar; the elements will be destroyed by fire, and the earth and everything in it will be laid bare" (2 Peter 3:10), illustrates the total destruction of the universe as we know it. Yet, there are hints that the new heaven and new earth have a relationship to the old, one of renewal rather than of annihilation and creation of an entirely new universe. To speak of a new heaven and a new earth is to speak about a renewed heaven and earth, no longer subject to decay, and freed from all evil—a true home of righteousness!

In John's vision, the new heaven and new earth have no sea. The chaos associated with the sea, the destruction, and the beasts associated with the sea (including the beast of Satan's power, Revelation 13:1–10) have been destroyed. The one who while on earth calmed the raging seas has shown His ultimate mastery over it. The chaos has been overcome, all sources of fear have been destroyed, and God's eternal peace is at hand.

To this new heaven and new earth descends the Holy City, the new Jerusalem, to be the dwelling place of God's people. Where the earthly Jerusalem, for all of its imperfections, was used by God to bring about our salvation, the new Jerusalem will be the perfect dwelling place of God and His people forever. The city is prepared as a bride, for the church, the people who will dwell in the city, is the bride of Christ, made pure and chaste by God. As He promised His people so often in the Old Testament and as He has promised us as well, we will be His people and He will be our God. God will be Immanuel, "God with us," in the fullest sense of that name. All pain, tears, mourning, and death will have been eliminated, for their source, the sin which divides person from person and people from God, will have been destroyed. All things truly will be made new, as full, joyful lives are lived out to their fullest potential, without sin getting in the way.

Now a voice speaks from the throne. The one who made everything in the beginning and has now made everything new tells John who will receive the gift of the new Jerusalem: those who are thirsty and come to the water of life, the gift won for us by Jesus Christ. Those who through the power of this water overcome the world and all of its trials will receive this as an inheritance. It is given to the heirs as a result of their relationship to their father. So, too, an inheritance comes by a death. In this case it is not the death of a father, but it is the death of the Son, who now empowers us to overcome the world. Those who continue to rebel against God will have no part in that age.

2. New Jerusalem Close Up (21:9–27)

One of God's angels now comes to John to show him the new Jerusalem, the bride of the Lamb, in more detail. (See figure 1.) Since the bride of Christ was purchased by His blood and is the dwelling place of the redeemed, the focus now turns from the theme of creation, God's making all things new, to redemption. To express the richness of this holy city, the city is described as a precious jewel, though it does not shine with its own radiance, but rather with the glory of God.

The perfection of the city is seen in the use of the number 12, for the Old Testament and New Testament church, the 12 tribes and the 12 apostles and 1,000, the cube of 10, signifying absolute completeness. The 12 gates to the city have the names of the 12 tribes, and the 12 foundations of the wall of the city have the names of the 12 apostles, showing that the church has indeed been built upon the foundation of the apostles and prophets

(Ephesians 2:20). At each gate stands an angel to welcome the people of God.

The perfection of the city is borne out by its measurements: It is a perfect cube of perfect size. The foundations of the walls are described in terms of precious stones. Each of the foundations, each decorated with one of these precious stones, bears the name of one of the apostles. To complete the picture of priceless value, we are told that each of the gates is made from a single pearl, and the great street of the city is made of gold. In both the tabernacle and in the temple, the Most Holy Place, the Holy of Holies, was built in the shape of a cube. All of God's people, the whole church, are now pure and spotless because of Christ.

Instead of a temple to signify God's presence among His people, a presence known only by faith, God has now chosen to make His dwelling among His people, so that He Himself now serves as the temple. The New Jerusalem itself is the Most Holy Place because God dwells there with a people whom He has made holy. Just as God showed His glory in the tabernacle and in the temple, so now His glory shines forth in the new Jerusalem. No other lights are needed. The people of all the nations, all from throughout the world whose names were written in

the Book of Life, will come to the city and will be welcomed at all times, for the gates will never be shut.

3. Life in New Jerusalem (22:1–6)

These final visions conclude with the angel showing John the river of the water of life, which flows through the middle of the city from the throne of God and the Lamb. The Lamb accomplishes the work for which the Father sent Him, and the Spirit, the river of life, brings the blessings of that work to each of God's people.

The final evidence of our complete reconciliation with God is seen in the reappearance of the tree of life. What was once forbidden to us because of our sin is now made available to us once again. That relationship which God intended us to have with Him from the beginning is ours once more. Every vestige of the curse of sin has been removed. Now it will be possible, indeed it will be our privilege, to look upon the face of God.

The angel's final words to John are ones of assurance and encouragement. God had sent him to show these things which would soon take place because that word can be trusted. God's people may now be prepared for what is to come, for they know their goal.

Our
Victorious Lord
Reigns Forever

Revelation 21:1–22:21

Resources for Worship

Use these resources for your daily study and at the week's assembly.

Hymn

1. Jerusalem the golden,
   With milk and honey blest,
   Beneath your contemplation
   Sink heart and voice oppressed.
   I know not, oh, I know not
   What joys await us there,
   What radiancy of glory,
   What bliss beyond compare.

2. They stand, those halls of Zion,
   Conjubilant with song
   And bright with many an angel
   And all the martyr throng.
   The prince is ever in them;
   The daylight is serene;
   The pastures of the blessed
   Are decked in glorious sheen.

3. There is the throne of David,
   And there, from care released,
   The shout of those who triumph,
   The song of those who feast.
   And they, who with their leader
   Have conquered in the fight,
   Forever and forever
   Are clad in robes of white.

4. Oh, sweet and blessed country,
   The home of God's elect!
   Oh, sweet and blessed country
   That eager hearts expect!
   In mercy, Jesus, bring us
   To that dear land of rest!
   You are, with God the Father
   And Spirit, ever blest.

(*Lutheran Worship* 309)

Prayer

Merciful Father, whose dear Son, our Lord Jesus Christ, rose Victor over death and the grave, we remember with thanksgiving Your faithful people who have trusted in Christ, whose tears are gone, and whose sorrows You have turned into joy; and we humbly implore You to strengthen us in the confident hope of the resurrection of the dead and the life of the world to come; through our Lord Jesus Christ. Amen.

Digging Deep
My Personal Study
for Week 9   *Revelation 21:1–22:21*

Day 1   Read Revelation 21:1–8

1. A new heaven and earth replaces the old when the Lord suddenly and unexpectedly brings about the destruction of this present universe (2 Peter 3:10–13). To indicate to us the nature of this new heaven and earth, we are told that there will no longer be any sea. What did the sea represent in the old earth?
a. Psalm 46:2–3

b. Luke 21:25

c. Revelation 13:1

2. We see the Holy City, the new Jerusalem, in which God's people will live. God says about life in this city, "I am making everything new" (v. 5). Read verses 3–4. Which aspect(s) of this newness seems most attractive to you?

3. God invites all who are thirsty to come to Him to be satisfied from the "spring of the water of life" (v. 6). What is meant by this imagery (John 4:13–14; John 7:38–39)?

4. Verse 8 presents a list of those who will be excluded from the heavenly city (see also 1 Corinthians 6:9–11). What do these sins reveal about those who persist in practicing them? (Consider Matthew 12:32; 23:37; John 3:19.)

Day 2   Read Revelation 21:9–27

5. Once again John is shown the new Jerusalem, which is now called "the bride, the wife of the Lamb" (v. 9). This is the church, the people of God (2 Corinthians 11:2; Ephesians 5:22–33), who are called into the close relationship of love that Christ has with His people. The city has 12 gates (v. 12), on which are written the names of the 12 tribes of Israel, and 12 foundations, on which are written the names of the 12 apostles. What does this tell us about the church in heaven? (Remember that the number 12 symbolizes the church.)

6. Each foundation of the city, upon which is written the name of one of the apostles, is made of a precious stone. A comparison with the list of precious stones (vv. 19–20) with the precious stones embedded on the breastplate worn by the high priest in the Old Testament (Exodus 28:15–21) includes most of the same stones, though there are some differences. Note that the names of the 12 tribes were written on the precious stones set in the high priest's breastplate. What does this compari-

son suggest to you about the glorified church in heaven? (See also 1 Peter 2:9.)

7. Note also that the city is a perfect cube (Revelation 21:16). The Most Holy Place of the Old Testament tabernacle and temple was also a cube. It was in the Most Holy Place, which no one might enter except the high priest (and he only once a year), that God dwelt in His glory. What does this correspondence of the shape of the city to the shape of the Most Holy Place tell us about the city? (See also Revelation 21:11, 22–23.)

8. Note the reasons why there will be no need to close the city gates (vv. 25–27). What is meant by the absence of night in the city (Romans 13:12–13)?

9. What about the descriptions in this chapter of life in heaven do you find most appealing?

Day 3   Read Revelation 22:1–5

10. Read Genesis 2:8–14. What similarities do you see between the Garden of Eden and the new heaven and the new earth of God's promise?

The Millennium and the Doom of Satan

Revelation 20:1–15

Among the most prevalent teachings on the Last Days is the expectation of the millennium, a thousand-year period in which Christ will rule the world before the final judgment and the end of the world. This view is called premillennialism, because its advocates declare that Christ will return before the millennium gets under way and will rule the nations from Jerusalem. (See figure 1.) Premillennialists believe that when Christ returns the believing dead will be raised to rule with Christ on earth, and that the world will continue with believers and unbelievers mixed together throughout the millennium. Satan will be bound so that God's people will hold sway in the world, while the ungodly, though continuing to live in the world, will find their power suppressed. The rule of Christ will result in the conversion of the bulk of the Jewish nation, and more people will come to faith during this time. At the end of the millennium Satan will be unleashed for the one final battle, in which he and his forces will finally be destroyed. Then the resurrection of the ungodly and of those who died during the millennium will take place, which will be the second resurrection. The ungodly will then be condemned and subjected to the "second death," that is, eternal death.

Though not common now, there also has existed in some parts of the church a teaching known as postmillennialism, which

promises that the teachings of Christ will slowly pervade the whole world so that the world will be substantially won for Christ. The present age will thereby gradually fade into a millennium in which Christianity will have so thoroughly permeated the world that evil will be suppressed virtually everywhere, and Christ will return to a world which will be for the most part Christian.

A period of "one thousand years" *is* mentioned in Revelation 20. However, in all of the recorded words of Christ concerning His return and in all of the other New Testament references to that event (1 Thessalonians 4, 1 Corinthians 15, and 2 Peter 3), there is no mention of a millennial reign of Christ on earth. The return of Christ is always spoken of with finality. The days before His return are referred to as the *last* days (2 Peter 3:3; 2 Timothy 3:1; Acts 2:17).

Though the term is not specifically used in Scripture of the day of Christ's return, the church has always recognized that these last days, stretching from Christ's ascension to His return, will culminate in the last *day*; the day in which Christ returns as judge. At that time heaven and earth will pass away. There will be no thousand-year period before that happens. A literal thousand-year reign of Christ on earth cannot be derived from the Scriptures at all and therefore not from Revelation 20. In fact, Christ is

quite adamant in declaring that His kingdom is not of this world (John 18:36).

1. Satan Bound for a Thousand Years (20:1–3)

The seventh and final vision begins with an angel coming down from heaven with the key to the Abyss, to hell itself, and holding a chain. The angel seizes the dragon, who is explicitly identified as Satan, and binds him for a thousand years. He is locked in the Abyss for the specific purpose of not allowing him to deceive the nations for this period. Since the number 1,000 signifies completeness, the thousand-year period is to be identified as the complete New Testament era, a specific length of time set and known only by God Himself. (See figure 2.) During this time Satan himself is not allowed to deceive the nations; that is, the Gospel is allowed free course throughout the world, and Satan can do nothing to prevent it.

Only at the end, at the time shortly before Christ's return, will he be released again for a short time and again be allowed to deceive the nations, and if it were possible, even the elect of God. That will be the time of great apostasy spoken of by Paul (2 Timothy 3:1–8) and by Christ Himself (Matthew 24:9–13, 21–25), as Satan seeks one last time to overthrow the kingdom of God. God uses and will continue to use Satan to show the consequences of sin, the evil

nature of this world's order, and ultimately His judgment against all sin and evil. Satan, for all of his bragging and his ferocity, can do only what God lets him do.

2. The First Resurrection (20:4–6)

The vision continues as the apostle sees thrones on which were seated those "given authority to judge," that is, all who have overcome, who have remained faithful (Revelation 3:21). Specifically mentioned are the souls of those who have been beheaded because of their testimony of Jesus and because of the Word of God. In an age of intense persecution, God assures His people through the apostle John that even those who have died for the faith, indeed especially those people, have the hope of reigning with Christ. These are the people who are said to come to life and reign with Christ for the thousand-year period. Since John specifically declares that it is the *souls* of those who were beheaded who live and reign with Christ, the living and reigning take place in heaven, and not on earth. As long as Christ reigns from heaven, seated at the right hand of the Father, His saints reign with Him. This living and reigning is called the "first resurrection." Since it is souls who live and reign, this first resurrection cannot be the return from physical death which will take place on the Last Day. Rather, it is conversion, for it is then that the believer "has crossed over from death to life" (John 5:24).

John goes on to note that the rest of the dead did not come to life until the thousand years were ended. Those who do not come to know Christ have remained in death. They have not partaken of the first resurrection, remaining separated from God, so that at the resurrection on the Last Day they will be restored only to physical life. Rather than experiencing the real life that God desires for all people, they will be subjected to the "second death," eternal separation from God, condemned and punished by Him forever.

3. The Final Battle (20:7–10)

At the end of the "thousand years," when Satan is released from his prison, he will again go out to deceive the nations. This will begin the great apostasy, as Satan gathers his forces and attempts one last time to overthrow Christ's rule. The battle mentioned here is the battle of Armageddon. The forces set against God are named Gog and Magog, names taken from Ezekiel 38–39. Magog is mentioned in Genesis 10:2 and in 1 Chronicles 1:5, which are genealogical tables, as a son of Japheth. The location of the actual, historical nation of Magog cannot be determined precisely, as the name does not occur again in the Scriptures until mentioned by Ezekiel, and then not again until Revelation 20.

In Revelation "Gog and Magog" are symbolic references to God's enemies in this world. As in Ezekiel, so in Revelation, God shows Himself to be completely in control of history. Though the enemies of God surround "the

city He loves" (believers, of which the physical city of Jerusalem is a representation), God will not allow it to be destroyed.

While in chapter 19 the focus was on the destruction of Satan's agents, the beast and the false prophet, that is, the Antichrist and anti-Spirit, his power and propaganda, now the focus is on the destruction of Satan himself. Satan is thrown into the lake of burning sulfur, the same lake used for the destruction of his agents, not to be annihilated, but to be punished forever.

4. The Judgment (20:11–15)

All of the dead, all of those who have ever lived on the earth, from Adam and Eve onward, have been raised to life, for even the sea has given up its dead, as have death and Hades themselves. All now stand before the judgment seat of God—and the books are opened. The accounts are laid bare, and each person is judged according to what he or she has done, according to what has been recorded in the books. The accounts of each person's activity are set before the world.

Jesus, as He relates the coming of the King for judgment in Matthew 25:31–46, also points to good works—how one has treated the members of His body, the church ("My brethren"). These works indicate faith as their basis, for only a Christian can serve fellow Christians in recognition that they are indeed members of Christ's family. So, while this judgment seemingly takes place on the basis of works, there is another, all important factor

The Millennium and the Doom of Satan

Revelation 20:1–15

STUDY 8

Resources for Worship

Use these resources for your daily study. They may be used again during the week's assembly.

Hymn

Do not despair, O little flock,
Although the foes' fierce battle shock
    Loud on all sides assail you!
Though at your fall they laugh, secure,
Their triumph cannot long endure;
    Let not your courage fail you!

The cause is God's; obey His call
And to His hand commit your all
    And fear no ill impending!
Though not yet seen by human eyes,
His Gideon shall for you arise,
    God's Word and you defending.

As sure as God's own Word is true,
Not Satan, hell, nor all their crew
    Can stand against His power.
Scorn and contempt their cup will fill,
For God is with His people still,
    Their help and their strong tower.

Then help us, Lord! Now hear our prayer.
Defend Your people ev'rywhere
    For Your own name's sake. Amen.
Then with a mighty hymn of praise
Your Church in earth and heav'n will raise
    Their songs of triumph. Amen.

(*Lutheran Worship* 300)
Copyright © 1978 *Lutheran Book of Worship*. By permission of Concordia Publishing House.

Reflection

This hymn, "Do Not Despair, O Little Flock," was sung in the morning devotions of the Lutheran soldiers under King Gustavus Adolphus of Sweden on Nov. 16, 1632. The king lost his life in the battle that day but the soldiers he had led won the battle.

Prayer

Keep in remembrance, O Lord, the tempted, the distressed, and the erring. Gently guide them and by Your great goodness bring them into the way of peace and truth. Let the light of Your truth shine on those who do not know You, that they may be turned toward You and so find peace. Graciously regard all who are in trouble, danger, temptation, bondage of sin, and those to whom death draws near. In Your mercy draw them to Yourself; for the sake of Jesus Christ, our Lord. Amen.

Digging Deep
My Personal Study
for Week 8   *Revelation 20:1–15*

Day 1   Read Revelation 20:1–3

1. An "angel" (a term that means "messenger") comes from heaven holding the key to hell (the Abyss) and a great chain. Refer back to Revelation 1:18. Who has the key to hell (death and Hades)—and by what right does that person hold the key?

2. With the chain the angel confines and binds Satan to prevent him from "deceiving the nations anymore until the thousand years are ended." During this time Satan himself cannot work directly, but works in the world through his agents, the ungodly powers that are operative in this world (the beast, the second beast, and the prostitute). When did this confining and binding take place (Hebrews 2:14; 1 John 3:8)?

3. Remember that in Revelation numbers have symbolic meanings, and the number 10 and its multiples represent completeness. One thousand is 10 cubed ($10 \times 10 \times 10$); it represents a complete period of time which God has determined. This period of time is the entire New Testament era, from Christ's death, resurrection, and ascension until the time when Christ comes again to judge all humankind. During this time Satan will not be able to prevent the spread of the Gospel to all the world. Summarize in your own words what is

happening during this period as Jesus describes it in Matthew 24:4–14.

4. What assurance does Jesus give to Christians concerning the devil and his forces?
a. Matthew 16:18.

b. John 10:27–29.

5. Summarize what will happen at the end of this age (Matthew 24:29–31; 25:31–35, 41).

Day 2   Read Revelation 20:4

6. John now views the situation of believers in this thousand-year period. What does the fact that John sees the "souls" of these believers suggest about where the believers are?

7. Find and jot down common themes from this verse that correspond with the following passages:
a. 2 Timothy 2:11–12a

b. 1 Corinthians 6:2–3a

c. Matthew 5:11–12

8. Note the phrase "they came to life and reigned with Christ a thousand years." Read John 5:24; 20:31; Ephesians 2:1,4–6. When might it be said that believers come to life?

9. What comfort or encouragement do you find in Revelation 20:4? (As you think about this question consider also Revelation 2:10.)

Day 3   Read Revelation 20:5–6

10. Unbelievers are said not to come to life until the thousand years were ended. In what way will unbelievers come to life when Christ comes again? (Read Daniel 12:2 and John 5:28–29.)

11. The time when believers come to life is called "the first resurrection" (v. 5b). For believers, then, there are two resurrections—a resurrection to life when they come to faith in Jesus and a resurrection of the body when Christ comes in His glory at the end of time. Only believers take part in the first

The Agony of the Wicked and the Ecstasy of the Saved

Revelation 17:1–19:21

The vision of the seven bowls showed the outpouring of God's wrath upon those who followed the beast, that is, upon rebellious humanity. The vision of the destruction of the beasts and the fall of Babylon, which causes great agony for the people of this world who attached themselves to her, is followed by another glimpse of heaven, where the saints of God utter ecstatic cries of praise to God for His salvation, as they celebrate the wedding supper of the Lamb.

1. A Woman Sitting on a Beast (17:1–18)

Chapter 17 opens with words showing that what is to be revealed here describes the events of the seventh bowl in more detail. The seventh bowl has begun the description of the final judgment, noting the reaction of the people of the world—the inhabitants of the earth—to God's judgment against them: rage and cursing against God. Now, one of the angels who poured out the bowls of wrath upon the world comes to John specifically to show him the judgment of God against Babylon. She is named Babylon, and like the historical city of Babylon (see figure 1), she sits upon "many waters" (Jeremiah 51:13), though the waters here represent all peoples, multitudes, nations, and languages (Revelation 17:15), rather than the Euphrates River and the elaborate network of irrigation canals that marked the historical city.

Like historical Babylon, this Babylon is also a "great city" (Revelation 17:18), so large that it dwarfs the comparative few who are God's chosen. She is portrayed as a prostitute seated upon the beast from the sea—the Antichrist, Satan's anti-Christian power. She is called the great prostitute because she entices humanity away from faithfulness to the true God to go lusting after herself. The rulers of the world ally themselves with her because in their eyes she has more to offer than God Himself does. For in this world the people of God bear crosses rather than crowns. Clothed in the riches of this world, she despises those who are clothed from above with the righteousness of Christ. Making herself alluring to the world, she is in fact an abomination in the eyes of God and His people.

In the Old Testament, the intimate relationship between God and his people is often compared to that of a husband and wife, and in the New Testament the imagery is transformed to show the relationship between Christ and His church. This image will be built upon in the vision of the marriage supper of the Lamb (Revelation 19:6–10), and reaches its culmination in Revelation 21:2, as the New Jerusalem, the City of God, comes down from heaven "prepared as a bride beautifully dressed for her husband."

The beast, on which the great prostitute sits, is the Antichrist, the one, who in imitation of the Lamb, is described as the one who "once was, now is not, and will come" (17:8), just as the Lamb who once was dead now lives (1:18; 2:8). He comes from out of the Abyss, the realm of Satan himself. The beast is described in terms of his activity in human history, as he continually works through the nations of the world to oppress God's people.

The description of the sevenfold kingdom may be a reference to the six great empires of the ancient world, from Egypt through Rome, the one who "now is," and with the seventh yet to come, who would endure for a little while, being all anti-Christian powers in the subsequent times. There will always be such kings in the world, who will seek to destroy the church. The eighth is the beast himself, who is the power behind the empires, the one who exercises the power of Satan to attack God's people in every generation. Though enduring through the ages of this world, he, too, is going to his destruction.

Who are the 10 kings to come? Ten is the number of completeness, therefore the number refers to all future kings of this world who ally themselves with the power of the Antichrist. They will endure for an hour, that is, like all earthly realms, they will last but a short time, and they,

too, will be destroyed. Ultimately, Babylon will be destroyed by the beast, who unwittingly serves as an agent of God's judgment.

2. The Fall of Babylon (18:1–24)

The historical city of Babylon, which oppressed the people of God and took them into captivity and exile, is the reference point for the Babylon of Revelation. Just as historical Babylon fell, never to rise again (Jeremiah 51:64), so also spiritual Babylon must ultimately fall and never rise again. Chapter 18 describes the fall from its announcement, to the reaction of the world, to the results and implications of that fall. In spite of what she is by nature, indeed even because of it, the nations of the world, the kings, and the merchants were enamored with her, because she gave them what they wanted. The people of God, who must live among her, are called upon by the voice of Christ Himself to come out of her. The Lord gives back to Babylon everything that she has dished out upon His people. She will be paid back double for her evil.

Those who closely attached themselves to Babylon will see her destruction and be terrified by it. Three groups are mentioned here—kings, merchants, and seamen. There is not a shred of penitence among them, nor is there any mention of the evils perpetrated by that city. Having had a part in the city and having partaken in her pleasures, a religion that made them feel good and gave them what they wanted, these people lament its destruction because it means an

end to their own wealth and well-being, and because it is a prelude to their own destruction.

The kings who committed adultery with her, who lay in the lap of her luxury, weep and mourn at the suddenness of her doom. In counterpoint to the words of those who lament the fall of Babylon, the angel narrating these events calls upon heaven and all of God's people on earth and heaven—saints, apostles, and prophets, to rejoice at the fall of Babylon, because God has now vindicated them. As for the servants of Babylon, they find themselves where there is only wailing and gnashing of teeth.

To conclude the scene, another angel appears and throws a millstone into the sea, declaring that Babylon will be cast down with violence. Looked at from one aspect, the words of the angel seem like words of lament similar to those of the kings, merchants, and seamen, but ultimately they are words of exultation that a city responsible for the deaths of so many of God's people has been so thoroughly destroyed that it will never rise again. Those who rejoice are people of God, not because of anything in themselves that makes them superior, but because by God's grace they repented and believed the Good News of salvation in Christ.

3. Rejoicing in Heaven (19:1–10)

Having been called upon to ... .e (Revelation 18:20), heaven responds with rejoicing, with shouts of "Hallelujah!" God is praised for all that is His—all

salvation, glory, and power. God has provided the victory over sin and evil; He alone possesses true majesty of His own; and He alone has the strength to subdue all of His enemies. All of these He shows as He judges all of creation and condemns the great prostitute.

The cry of the martyrs for vindication, issued in Revelation 6:9–11, has finally been answered, and God's people have been avenged. To the cry of this multitude that no one can number, the 24 elders (the church as a whole) and the four living creatures (all of creation) respond, "Amen, Hallelujah!" That well-known Hebrew word "Amen" simply means, "Yes, it is true." To that affirmation they add their own word of praise.

The voice from the throne then calls upon the multitude to expand upon that song of praise, calling them "His servants," and including both the small and the great. To this exhortation the multitude responds with another "Hallelujah!" rejoicing that the time for the wedding of the Lamb has come. The Bridegroom has come to take His bride into His house, where she will live with Him forever.

The bride of the Lamb, which is the church, has been prepared for the wedding. She is clothed in fine linen, which we are told stands for the righteous acts of the saints. Only those who have been clothed in Christ's righteousness are able to wear such righteous acts. The angel now instructs John to write the fourth beatitude: "Blessed are those who are invited to the wedding supper of the Lamb!"

The Agony of the Wicked and the Ecstasy of the Saved

Revelation 17:1–19:21

STUDY 7

Resources for Worship

Use these resources for your daily study. They may be used again during the week's assembly.

Hymn

The day is surely drawing near
  When Jesus, God's anointed,
In all His power shall appear
  As judge whom God appointed.
Then fright shall banish idle mirth,
And hungry flames shall ravage earth
  As Scripture long has warned us.

The final trumpet then shall sound
  And all the earth be shaken,
And all who rest beneath the ground
  Shall from their sleep awaken.
But all who live will in that hour,
By God's almighty, boundless pow'r,
  Be changed at His commanding.

May Christ our intercessor be
  And through His blood and merit
Read from His book that we are free
  With all who life inherit.
Then we shall see Him face to face,
With all His saints in that blest place
  Which He has purchased for us.

O Jesus Christ, do not delay,
  But hasten our salvation;
We often tremble on our way
  In fear and tribulation.
Oh, hear and grant our fervent plea;
Come, mighty judge, and set us free
  From death and ev'ry evil.

(*Lutheran Worship* 462)

Prayer

O God, so rule and govern our hearts and minds by Your Holy Spirit that, being ever mindful of the eventual end of all things and the agony of the wicked and the ecstasy of the saved on the day of Your just judgment, we may be stirred up to ever stronger faith and holiness of living here, and hereafter dwell with You forever in heaven, through Jesus Christ, Your Son, our Lord, who lives and reigns with You and the Holy Spirit, ever one God, world without end. Amen.

Digging Deep
My Personal Study
for Week 7   *Revelation 17:1–19:21*

Unlike earlier visions that describe events during the whole time between Christ's ascension and His return in glory, this vision concentrates on the final judgment of "Babylon" and those who have joined themselves with her.

Day 1   Read Revelation 17:1–18

1. The great enemy of God in this world is described as a prostitute, and those people who have cooperated with this enemy and have joined in opposing God and His church are said to have committed adultery with the prostitute. In the Old Testament idolatry is sometimes described as adultery (for example, Judges 2:11, 17). How do you think idolatry (giving any created thing the regard that is due only to God) might be said to be a spiritual adultery?

2. a. Note the seductive appearance of the prostitute (Revelation 17:4a). How do you think ungodly powers are seductive in appealing to people in our present age?

b. *For personal meditation only.* Think about the seductive appeal of temptation and the gradual way it leads us, stage by stage, into sin, as described in verse 2 ("intoxicated") and James 1:14–15. Think through this sequence as it applies to a specific sin or temptation that you've been wrestling with. Then ask your Father in heaven, for Jesus' sake, to give you strength to resist and overcome that temptation. Finally, hear His word of forgiveness and power as you meditate on Romans 13:11–14 and 1 Corinthians 10:13.

3. The prostitute is described as sitting on a beast having seven heads (which represent the seven hills upon which the woman sits and also seven kings—perhaps past, present, and future rulers of the Roman empire) and 10 horns (representing 10 kings—perhaps future rulers in this world). The city of Rome was originally built on seven hills and was ruled by a succession of rulers. These rulers, and the kings to come, represent the power with which the prostitute rules in this world. But the Roman Empire in the time of the apostles was only part of what is represented by the prostitute. She represents the seductiveness of the anti-church that Satan sets up in this world. What is the goal of the prostitute in employing her seductive power (vv. 13–14)?

4. As we have seen previously in our study, the rulers of the Roman Empire promoted a worship of the Roman emperor as a god by requiring that people burn incense before the image of the emperor as an act of worship. (The reference to the beast in verses 8 and 11 as "once was, now is not, and will come up . . . " attempts to imitate God and to lay claim to divinity.) How do you think rulers today have required (or might require) people to do things that are disloyal to God?

5. The prostitute rules over "peoples, multitudes, nations and languages" (v. 15). The Roman empire took in many different nations and peoples. But these subjects of the prostitute will rebel against her and destroy her as they act, though unintentionally, under the direction of God's will. Give some examples from your experience or from

history that illustrate how God guides the course of events (often without the awareness of those involved as to what God is doing) to achieve His purpose (v. 17).

Day 2   Read Revelation 18:1–20

6. An angel appears to make an announcement concerning "Babylon." The angel speaks with great authority. He comes from heaven and has a splendor that illuminates the earth.
a. What does Exodus 34:29–35 suggest to you about the reason for that illuminating splendor?

b. Consider the angel's message (vv. 2–3). Remember that when John received and revealed this message, the enemies of Christ were still very much in power in this world. How comforting and encouraging this message must have been to the Christians then contending with ungodly powers and seductive temptations! What are some affirmations of the faith that are especially precious to you that you believe on the strength of God's authoritative Word, even though these affirmations have not yet been fulfilled? (For thought starters, read such passages as Isaiah 11:6–9, Romans 8:18, and 1 Corinthians 15:51–54.)

7. In verse 4 another voice from heaven admonishes Christians in John's day (and ours, too, of course) to come out from the ungodly forces that surround us (see also 1 Peter 5:8–9). How do you

Praise for God and Armageddon for the World

Once again it is important to remember that the events described here cover the entire New Testament era, from Christ's ascension until His return. The focus, however, now turns specifically to the wrath of God, His holy and righteous anger against a disobedient and disbelieving humanity.

1. Appearance of the Seven Angels (15:1–8)

As with the visions of the seals and trumpets, the scene begins in heaven as preparations are made for the pouring out of the seven last plagues, which complete the wrath of God. Once again, the people of God who have come through the great tribulation, described as "victorious over the beast," stand at the sea of glass (see 4:6). Their victory over the beast looks to the world like defeat, for they won that victory by dying. Thus they followed the example of the Lamb, whose death is the source of their victory, and whose resurrection made that victory apparent.

The song the saints sing is described as "the song of Moses and the song of the Lamb." The Old Testament describes two songs of Moses: the first recorded in Exodus 15:1–18, the second recorded in Deuteronomy 32. Both songs declare God's power and God's sovereignty over history and declare God's victory over His enemies. Both declare that in the end all nations will recognize

that the Lord is God. But the song they sing is also the "Song of the Lamb." As Moses was the first deliverer of Israel, leading them to the Promised Land, so the Lamb, the last deliverer, through His death and resurrection has led His people to eternal life. The song of the Lamb, sung to the Lamb and about the Lamb, proclaims the eternal deliverance of God's people from all of their enemies, including death itself.

The Tabernacle of the Testimony is opened, and the seven angels with the seven plagues come out. Dressed in linen and wearing golden sashes, they serve as mediators of God's punishment to the world. As the tabernacle in the wilderness and the temple in Jerusalem served to point to the presence of God among His people in the Old Testament, so the heavenly temple does so here. The smoke, which is the glory of God, appears, making God's presence among his people known as it did in the Old Testament. Since no sinful human can see God and live, and since no one can stand under the righteous wrath of the most holy God, no one is allowed in the temple until the pouring out of God's wrath is completed.

2. The Seven Bowls of Wrath (16:1–21)

The angels are then sent out to pour the bowls of God's wrath out upon the earth. (See figure 1.) As the plagues against the

Egyptians showed God's judgment against an unbelieving people who had enslaved God's people, so the plagues of the seven bowls are directed exclusively against the unbelieving world. As with the previous visions, the events described take place throughout the age of the church. The plagues mentioned are sent both to drive people to repentance and ultimately to punish those who refuse to repent.

The first bowl is poured out on the land. Sores break out on the people who worshiped the beast and had his mark upon them, reminiscent of the sixth plague poured out on Egypt, in which boils and abscesses broke out upon the people. Those who follow the beast and worship his power will in the end find that their hopes are fruitless and their spirits in agony as they realize that the powers of this world will pass away and only God and His own endure forever.

The second plague affects the waters of the sea. The third plague affects the waters of the land—rivers and springs. In both cases, the waters turn to blood, as did the waters of the Nile in the first of the plagues with which the Lord struck Egypt (Exodus 7:14–24). The result is death—death to every living thing in the sea, and death to those who have put God's people to death. The angel in charge of the waters notes the justice of God's judgment as He

tailors the punishment to fit the crime. Those who have shed the blood of the saints are now forced to drink blood. Rejecting the blood of Christ, they instead shed the blood of His servants. They are forced to drink the blood of God's wrath that runs through the rivers of the land.

The fourth bowl is poured out on the sun. The sun then sends forth its fire to strike the people. While these fires are not yet the fires of eternal punishment, they are a foretaste of that punishment. One of the purposes is still to bring people to repentance, but it will not have that effect. Rather than acknowledging error, human self-righteousness defies God to the end. Knowing that it is God who is striking them, they turn and blaspheme God for giving them what they deserve.

The fifth angel pours out his bowl on the throne of the beast and plunges it into darkness. Even before this age comes to an end, the agents of Satan will be shown to be powerless. Though thought to be the one who offers all of the blessings of power and prosperity, Satan's throne will be plunged into darkness, and his followers will as well. His followers realize that they have nothing left for themselves but the pain of the "outer darkness" a sense of abandonment and utter hopelessness. Yet they will still refuse to repent, even in the midst of their pain.

The angel with the sixth bowl pours it out on the Euphrates, the river which marks the traditional eastern boundary between the lands of the Gentiles and the Promised Land

(Genesis 15:18; Deuteronomy 1:7). The nations of the East were the traditional enemies of the people of God—the ones who sought to destroy the nation completely: Assyria, Babylon, Persia.

The invasion now is a spiritual invasion; demonic spirits looking like frogs (listed among the unclean animals for the Jews in Leviticus 11:10) come out of the mouths of the beasts and the dragon. Speaking their lying words and performing their lying wonders, they entice the kings of the world to do battle against the people of God. Gathering together for battle, they expect to destroy, but that battle will in fact inaugurate their own end.

Here Christ warns His people that, though He will win the battle, His own people need to be prepared. Jesus warns His people to be prepared to flee the invasion to come, using the forthcoming battle which would lead to the destruction of Jerusalem as a foreshadowing of the great spiritual battle for human souls as the age draws to a close. Those not prepared will be exposed to destruction, but those who keep watch and are prepared for the end are called "blessed." This is the third beatitude.

The place of this great spiritual battle is named Armageddon. The name means "Mountain of Megiddo." The Plain of Megiddo was a significant strategic site in Israel. Though there is no specific mountain by that name, one of the most significant mountains in that region is Mount Carmel, the mountain

where God through Elijah defeated the priests of Baal.

Armageddon is clearly a spiritual battle, in which the enemies of God gather against His people for the final confrontation, at which time God intervenes directly to bring about the destruction of His enemies. That destruction takes place as the seventh bowl is poured out. The voice from the throne then thunders, "It is done!" and God makes His presence known.

The lightning, thunder, and earthquakes always signal the presence of the majesty of God. But while at Sinai they announced the covenant; at Armageddon they announce judgment. This earthquake brings about the destruction of Babylon itself and of all of the cities of the nations. God will unleash His full fury upon the world, and the result will be its total destruction.

Some popular books dealing with the End Times treat all of the events mentioned here, including the battle of Armageddon, as literal, physical events that will happen immediately before the end and go so far as to say that the things described are such that they could not have occurred until the present era. Such interpretations go contrary to the tenor of the entire book of Revelation, which quite clearly declares itself to be symbolic. To become preoccupied with timetables concerning the events of the end distracts the Christian from remembering the true purpose of the signs—to remind Christians in all ages that Christ is coming soon. The signs are

<table>
<tr><td>

Praise for God and Armageddon for the World

Revelation 15:1–16:21

</td><td>

STUDY 6

</td></tr>
</table>

Resources for Worship

Use these resources for your daily study. They may be used again during the week's assembly.

Hymn

"Wake, awake, for night is flying,"
The watchmen on the heights are crying;
    "Awake, Jerusalem, arise!"
Midnight hears the welcome voices
And at the thrilling cry rejoices:
    "Where are the virgins, pure and wise?
The bridegroom comes, awake!
Your lamps with gladness take!
    Alleluia!
With bridal care
And faith's bold prayer,
    To meet the bridegroom, come, prepare!"

Zion hears the watchmen singing,
And in her heart new joy is springing.
    She wakes, she rises from her gloom.
For her Lord comes down all glorious,
The strong in grace, in truth victorious,
    Her star's arising light has come!
"Now come, O blessed one,
Lord Jesus, God's own Son.
    Hail! Hosanna!
We answer all
In joy Your call,
    We follow to the wedding hall."

Now let all the heav'ns adore You,
Let saints and angels sing before You
    With harp and cymbals' clearest tone.
Of one pearl each shining portal,
Where, joining with the choir immortal,
    We gather round Your radiant throne.
No eye has seen that light,
No ear the echoed might
    Of Your glory;
Yet there shall we
In Your vict'ry
    Sing shouts of praise eternally!

(*Lutheran Worship* 177)

Reflection

Christians should daily raise the personal question, "What if Judgment Day or my death should come today? Am I prepared and ready?"

Prayer

Lord Jesus, help us to recognize how suddenly tribulation and trials can come upon us and how weak and frail we are to stand up against them. Keep us strong in faith that we may never be overcome by the weight of our affliction and thus despair in fear and grief. Help us to remember that all things work together for good to them that love You, our Savior and our Lord. Amen.

Digging Deep
My Personal Study
for Week 6   *Revelation 15:1–16:21*

Another vision reveals what will happen on the earth before Christ returns in glory. This vision enables us to see how the wrath of God is poured out upon unbelievers. Despite experiencing God's wrath, however, these unbelievers still will not look to God in repentance and faith.

Day 1   Read Revelation 15:1–4

1. *For personal meditation. Sharing optional.* Once again our attention is directed to the throne of God in heaven, and to two groups—seven angels (v. 1) and (v. 2) believers who were victorious over the beast (those powers in this world that serve the purposes of Satan, 13:1–10), the beast's image (the idolatry and false worship promoted by false teachings and satanic influences, 13:14–15), and the beast's number (the pressure exerted to give in to the power of Satan and to cooperate with his purposes, 13:16–18). Prayerfully read Ephesians 6:10–18, God's Word to you on achieving victory over these demonic forces. Then, as verse 18 suggests, "pray in the Spirit" to God "with all kinds of prayer and requests," especially "praying for all the saints." Think about and pray for members of your LifeLight group, family, or other Christians who may be facing fierce and subtle temptations that try their faith.

2. The saints in heaven sing "the song of Moses the servant of God and the song of the Lamb" (v. 3). Two songs of Moses are recorded in the Old Testament.
a. Scan Exodus 15:1–18. What is the theme of this song?

b. Scan the song of Moses recorded in Deuteronomy 32:1–43. What is the theme of this song?

3. Now read again the song recorded in Revelation 15:3–4. In what ways does this song reflect the songs of Moses in Exodus 15 and Deuteronomy 32?

Day 2   Read Revelation 15:5–8

4. The seven angels come out of the heavenly temple, or tabernacle, signifying that they were doing God's bidding and carrying out a mission He had given them. Notice how the angels are dressed and compare with Exodus 28:40. What do the priestly garments worn by the angels tell us about their mission?

5. The angels bring the seven plagues from the temple, yet receive the seven bowls filled with God's wrath from the four living creatures (which represent creation). This shows that God's wrath is being exercised through the created world.
a. How was God's judgment against the sin committed by Adam and Eve carried out through nature (Genesis 3:17–19)?

b. What does Paul say in Romans 8:19–21 about the role of the natural world in exercising God's anger against sin?

6. The smoke that fills the temple represents God's power and glory. Note the parallel between Revelation 15:8 and Exodus 40:34–35.
a. Why were not even Moses or the priests allowed to enter the temple when God was present in His glory (Isaiah 6:5 and 59:2)?

b. When will this situation change for believers (Colossians 3:4)?

Day 3   Read Revelation 16:1–7

7. The first three plagues, like the plagues set in motion by some of the seven trumpets in an earlier vision (8:7–12), are reminiscent of plagues inflicted upon Egypt through Moses and Aaron.

Christ's Victory over Satan and His Hosts

Revelation 12:1–14:20

Satan has two forces under his control which he uses in his efforts to gain control of the lives of the people of this world. One of these is raw power. He seeks to gain as many followers for himself as he can by force, seeking to drive people away from God and into his service. The other is his propaganda, in which he seeks to show the world that he, and not Christ, is worthy of worship. Even more subtly, he may seek to use the name of Christ Himself to bring about his ends. He will often masquerade as an "angel of light" (2 Corinthians 11:14), claiming to be a servant of God, as he uses his own false teachings to deceive people and lure them away from the kingdom of God.

The message is clear: Be on your guard and resist the power and deceit of Satan, for those who succumb will be destroyed by the wrath of God. But be assured also that God will remain faithful to His people, and will not allow them to be destroyed. He will preserve them from the fiercest onslaughts of Satan and his hosts.

1. The Dragon—Satan (12:1–17)

This set of seven visions begins with a vision in the heavens of a woman clothed in the sun and of a dragon. The woman is about to give birth, and the dragon waits to devour the child once he is born. After the child is born the woman goes into the wilderness

for 1,260 days (three and a half years), where God takes care of her. Since the woman wears a crown of 12 stars, the sign of the believing community, she undoubtedly represents God's faithful people. Christ, who is the Son of God and the Son of Mary, was born out of God's believing people, those who looked for the coming of the Savior.

The dragon, who is Satan (12:9), is a powerful adversary, as noted by his seven heads and 10 horns, which point to his great wisdom and power. The crowns on his head are *diadems,* crowns which represent deity. By wearing such crowns, he shows his own aspirations to deity, his desire to supplant God as the ruler of the universe. He waits to devour Christ and prevent Him from saving His people. (See figure 1.)

Yet in spite of these attempts, Christ was preserved in His task, and when it was completed He was "snatched up to God" (12:5), that is, He ascended into heaven. God's believing people, the church, has "fled into the desert" (12:6). She is in exile from her home, which is heaven. The time of this exile is 1,260 days, three and a half years. This is the time of persecution, during which God provides a place of refuge for His people, that is, keeps them under His care even in the midst of tribulation.

From here the scene switches to heaven, as Michael and his

angels strive against Satan and his hosts. Satan is ultimately defeated and decisively cast from heaven. Satan has not given up. He now turns his attention to earth, where he seeks to drive as many away from Christ as possible. Nevertheless, God's elect remain under His protection no matter how fierce the attacks of Satan become. Unable to destroy the believing community as a whole, Satan turns his attention to the rest of her offspring, that is, individual believers, those who joyfully keep God's commands and testify of Jesus, and seeks to destroy them one by one.

2. The First Beast—Anti-Christian World Powers (13:1–10)

Satan makes use of two beasts under his control. As the dragon, Satan, stands by the sea, he summons the first beast, who, like the dragon, has seven heads and 10 horns, and the crowns that he is wearing are diadems. For John's first readers, the anti-Christian world power that they were forced to contend with was Rome itself, whose head, the emperor, had aspirations to deity. People in every age have had to suffer such warfare, whether the empire be pagan Rome, Islamic Arabia, or the communist Soviet Union. When one such empire falls, another always seems to rise to take its place.

That amazing resiliency is seen in the fatal wound that has been

healed. Just as Christ died and rose, just as the church (though seemingly dead at times) continues to live, so also Satan's anti-Christian power will imitate God's ways, and seemingly be destroyed from time to time only to arise again in a new form.

The beast as described here combines the characteristics of the four beasts of Daniel 7:4–6. The beasts that Daniel saw represented the empires that would arise between his time and the birth of Christ. (See figure 2 in review leaflet 4.) The beast that John sees shows that the same anti-Christian power will be at work until God brings this age to its close. This beast blatantly blasphemes God, defying God and His people by bringing disgrace upon God and bringing death to God's people. People are attracted to power, and the great power of this beast will cause all of the inhabitants of the earth, that is, all those whose names are not written in the Book of Life, to worship it. While the beast exercises authority for 42 months (again, three and a half years, a period of time limited by God), God's people know that faithful endurance amid the harshest persecution will result in eternal life.

3. The Second Beast— Anti-Christian Propaganda (13:11–18)

The second beast is Satan's anti-Christian propaganda. This beast has two horns like a lamb, but speaks like a dragon (13:11); that is, he masquerades as Christ, but his words are the words of Satan. His purpose is to make the earth and its inhabitants worship the first beast. Thus he functions as an anti-Spirit. He works through the use of false miracles, "lying wonders." These counterfeit miracles are imitations of true miracles performed by God's prophets. These false signs deceive the inhabitants of the earth into worshiping the first beast, so that they set up an image in honor of that beast, the false Christ who seemed to be fatally wounded but yet lived.

Try as he will, Satan will not be able to deceive God's elect. Those whom the beast cannot convert he will seek to destroy. The beast forces a mark upon all of his followers, a mockery of the seal God has put on his people. As God's people bear the name of Christ, so the worshipers of the beast bear his name and number. The number of the beast is given as 666. The number may be understood in terms of the type of symbolism that is being used throughout the book. The number six may be understood as a falling short of perfection, one less than perfect seven. As 777 would express the perfection of the Trinity, 666 would express the falling short of perfection of the Anti-Trinity. Those who do not possess the "mark of the beast" will be oppressed economically—they will not be able to buy or sell without the "mark of the beast." Those who are opposed to Christ will use all the force at their disposal to make life difficult for God's people, including starving them. There are times when God's people will suffer for their faith. God does not promise deliverance from such trials. He *does* promise to bring us through them to Himself.

4. God's Victory Assured (14:1–13)

The final victory of God's people in spite of Satan's fiercest attacks is noted as the scene shifts from an earth in which the agents of Satan are triumphant to Mount Zion, the heavenly Jerusalem, where Jesus stands with the 144,000, the totality of His people. These are those who had the seal of Christ on their foreheads rather than the mark of the beast. They are "blameless"; their sins have been covered by the blood of Christ, and having come through death, they now stand spotless before God (Ephesians 5:27; Jude 24).

The scene now shifts away from heaven and back to earth. We now see three angels and hear their messages. The first angel calls the world to repent and to turn to the true God. As long as this age endures, the message will not be silenced, and God will continue to call people out of the world to Himself. The second angel calls out, "Fallen is Babylon the Great!" The anti-Christian powers of the world will meet their doom. Babylon, the great military power of the sixth century before Christ, had invaded Jerusalem, destroyed the temple, and deposed the king. Yet within 70 years Babylon itself had fallen; Israel was restored to its land.

Now Rome was doing the same. The similarity of Rome to Babylon was so great that Babylon had become a code word for Rome among Christians (1 Peter 5:13). All of the powers exemplified by Babylon will ultimately be destroyed. The

Christ's Victory over Satan and His Hosts

Revelation 12:1–14:20

Resources for Worship

Use these resources for your daily study. They may be used again during the week's assembly.

Hymn

A mighty fortress is our God,
A trusty shield and weapon;
He helps us free from ev'ry need
That hath us now o'ertaken.
The old evil foe
Now means deadly woe;
Deep guile and great might
Are his dread arms in fight;
On earth is not his equal.

With might of ours can naught be done,
Soon were our loss effected;
But for us fights the valiant One,
Whom God Himself elected.
Ask ye, Who is this?
Jesus Christ it is,
Of sabaoth Lord,
And there's none other God
He holds the field forever.

Though devils all the world should fill,
All eager to devour us,
We tremble not, we fear no ill,
They shall not overpow'r us.
This world's prince may still
Scowl fierce as he will,
He can harm us none,
He's judged; the deed is done;
One little word can fell him.

The Word they still shall let remain
Nor any thanks have for it;
He's by our side upon the plain
With His good gifts and Spirit.
And take they our life,
Goods, fame, child, and wife,
Though these all be gone,
Our vict'ry has been won;
The Kingdom ours remaineth.

(*Lutheran Worship* 298)

Prayer

Grant, O Lord, that when we are tempted, we may resist the old evil foe, the devil; that when we are worried, we may cast all our care upon You; that when we are weary, we may seek the refreshing rest which You alone can give us; so that in all things we may live this day and every day to Your glory; through Jesus Christ, our victorious Lord and Savior. Amen.

Digging Deep
My Personal Study
for Week 5 *Revelation 12:1–14:20*

The fourth vision begins. Like the second and third visions, this vision tells us what will happen until Christ comes again to bring this present age to an end. This vision, however, takes us back before time and this world began as it reveals the origin and nature of the devil's opposition to God and His believing people.

Day 1 Read Revelation 12:1–17

1. **Challenge Question.** Today's reading tells us how and why the devil came to be opposed to God and His believing people. The scene shifts back and forth between earth and heaven and back to earth again. First we are presented with a woman about to give birth and a dragon waiting to devour her child.

a. Read verse 1 and compare it with Genesis 37:9–11, where Joseph's father (Jacob, or Israel) and mother and 11 brothers (the forefathers of the tribes of the nation of Israel) are represented in Joseph's dream as sun, moon, and 11 stars. (Note also Revelation 12:17, and remember that the number 12 is the symbolic number of the church.) Using these clues, identify the woman about to give birth.

b. Read Revelation 12:5 and Psalm 2:4–9. Identify the child.

c. Read Revelation 12:3, 9. Who is the dragon?

2. a. What becomes of the woman's son (v. 5; John 14:2; Acts 1:2, 9)?

b. **Challenge Question.** What becomes of the woman (v. 6; John 17:11, 15)? (Remember that 1,260 days, or three and a half years, represent the limited period of time the devil is given to persecute the church.)

3. Now the scene shifts to heaven—and to an event that happened before the events symbolically referred to in verses 1–6—to tell us how the devil came to oppose the church on earth. We read of "war in heaven," when Michael and his angels fight against Satan and his angels. How is Michael identified in Jude 9?

4. a. When Satan is defeated and thrown out of heaven, he lands on earth. How is this both good news and bad news (Revelation 12:12)?

b. **Challenge Question.** What caused the war in heaven? Read Isaiah 14:12–15 (note that the phrase "O morning star" is translated "Lucifer" in Latin); Ezekiel 28:14–19; and Luke 10:18.

5. Frustrated in his efforts to win in heaven (vv. 7–12), and frustrated in his efforts to destroy God's Son (vv. 1–6), Satan now makes war against the church on earth.
a. Nevertheless, what assurance do you find in verses 14, 16, and in Matthew 16:18b?

b. What assurance is given to you personally in Luke 12:32 and in 2 Thessalonians 3:3?

Day 2   Read Revelation 13:1–10

As Satan had his allies in his war in heaven, so he has his allies as he makes war against the church on earth. In this reading we learn about one of these powerful allies. Like the dragon, the beast has seven heads (great wisdom) and 10 horns (tremendous power).

6. God gave the Old Testament prophet Daniel a vision that foretold how four empires would arise in succession. You may read this prophecy in Daniel 7:2–7, 15–22. You may also refer to the chart, figure 2 in review leaflet 4. Notice that the first beast has characteristics of these empires. Notice also what is said about the beast in Revelation 13:4, 7. These clues lead us to identify the beast as evil world powers in opposition to God and His people. Give examples from history of such oppression.

7. Give examples from history and life today—both crass and subtle—of the beast showing its arrogance against God by allowing itself to be worshiped and by proud words and blasphemies (vv. 4, 5, 8).

8. What penalties threatened those who would not join in worshiping the beast (v. 10a)?

9. Verse 10b tells us how we are called to respond to these threatened penalties. How can Paul's attitude as he faced the probability of giving up his life as a penalty for his faithfulness to Christ help and encourage you as you give your life for the Lord (2 Timothy 4:6–8)?

The World Shaken, God's Kingdom Stands Firm

Revelation 8:1–11:19

As we look at the series of visions presented in Revelation, it is tempting to see them standing in succession to one another. However, when we look at Christ's description of things to come as He explains them in the gospels and compare His words to the visions presented to John and recorded here, it becomes clear that these visions do not describe a series of judgments poured out on the world one after the other; rather, each vision describes the history of the world from Christ's ascension into heaven until the end of the world, each from a different standpoint. The vision of the seven trumpets looks at the same history from the standpoint of the judgment of God upon the world. Again the world is seen to be falling apart. This time, however, God's hand is seen bringing judgment upon the world because of human sin.

1. A Golden Censer (8:1–5)

The opening of the seventh seal inaugurates the next vision, that of the seven trumpets. The opening of the seal is greeted with silence. Now the preparations take place in heaven for the drama which will be played out on earth. Seven angels are handed seven trumpets. The seven angels, the messengers around the throne who do God's bidding, are called upon to announce the seven aspects of the judgment of God which make up God's complete judgment upon the world.

But before the sound of the trumpets begins, yet another angel comes, bringing a censer, who offers incense to God, which ascends to God with the prayers of the saints. As the prayers of the saints in heaven and on earth again are brought before God, calling for vindication and for justice, God begins to bring about His judgment upon the world. The angel with the censer fills it with fire from the altar and hurls it to earth, and lightning, thunder, and quaking earth foreshadow God's actions against an evil world. Then, one by one, the trumpets are sounded.

2. The First Four Trumpets (8:6–13)

The parallels between the events following the trumpet blasts and the plagues which God visited upon Egypt indicate that through these events God is preparing to free His people from their bondage in this world and lead them out of the world to the home He has promised them. (See figure 1.) One third of the earth, trees, and grass are burned up. These events occur to serve as a warning to the world about the strength of God's anger and the coming severity of His judgment but are not yet God's complete judgment.

At the sound of the second trumpet, a fiery mountain is cast into the sea, a third of which then turns to blood, an act reminiscent of the first plague on

Egypt (Exodus 7:20–21). Now, a third of the creatures living in the sea are destroyed, and a third of the ships on the seas. Again, the judgment is severe, but it is not final.

At the sound of the third trumpet, a blazing star falls to earth, which turns a third of the fresh water on earth bitter, that is, makes it undrinkable, leading to the death of many who drank it. In the wilderness, God sweetened the bitter waters at Marah (Exodus 15:25) as a sign for His people. Here, He turns sweet water bitter as a sign against those who reject Him.

At the sound of the fourth trumpet, the signs of God's judgment touch the sky. A third of the sun, the moon, and the stars are darkened. God put the lights in the sky as a sign to mark the days and the seasons (Genesis 1:14); now they serve as a sign that God has the power to bring the seasons to an end, further undermining human security in this life. The events here also call to mind the ninth plague on Egypt, the plague of darkness (Exodus 10:21–23).

The land, the waters of the sea, the waters of the land, and indeed the very heavens themselves have declared God's judgment. People have been affected only as a result of these phenomena in nature. But now things are going to change. An eagle flies through the air, with a cry, "Woe, woe, woe!" The cry of the eagle declares that the three

final trumpets will usher in a series of calamities far worse than the ones that have gone before and that these acts of judgment will strike human beings directly.

3. The Final Trumpets (9:1–21)

As the events of the final trumpets unfold, we see God unleashing the forces of evil upon the world. These forces will plague the world with increasing intensity, but they will do so only at God's command. At the sound of the fifth trumpet, a star, serving as an agent of God, falls to earth, with a key to open the Abyss, hell itself. Though the Abyss is the demons' place of confinement, God at His pleasure may allow them to work on earth, but their power is limited to what God will allow. They are instruments of God's judgment. God can use even His enemies to bring about His will.

Smoke arises from the Abyss, which darkens the sun. Out of the smoke comes a plague of locusts. Locusts had been a sign of God's judgment upon Egypt at the time of Moses (Exodus 10:1–20, the eighth plague), and by the prophets Amos (Amos 7:1–3) and Joel (Joel 1:2–2:11). Their "king" is known as the Destroyer, yet this king has no real power, for it is God who has released them, and it is God who sets the limits of their power. These locusts strike only people without God's seal, so that they suffer but do not die. They are allowed to plague humanity for five months, a period of time suggested by the life cycle of the locust.

The sound of the sixth trumpet brings the second woe. Now four angels who are in charge of a vast army are released to kill one third of humanity. God allows the demonic hordes to do their work, even to bring about death, but for His own purposes. His purposes include not only judgment, but also repentance. Nevertheless, even in the face of destruction, people will of their own accord remain attached to the very things that have brought destruction upon them.

4. The Little Scroll (10:1–11)

Now an angel appears with a little scroll. This angel is described with images of God's covenant with His people: the rainbow given to Noah, the pillars of cloud and fire that led Israel through the wilderness, the face shining as the sun as did the face of Jesus at His transfiguration.

This angel, planting one foot on the land and the other on the sea, showing that his message affects the destiny of all of creation, gives a shout. At his shout the seven thunders, the complete judgment of God, speak. Yet the time for that judgment has not yet come, and so their words are sealed up until that time. Six trumpets have sounded, and God's mystery will be fulfilled when the seventh and final trumpet is about to sound.

Now, however, John is to take the little scroll and eat it. This scroll tastes sweet in John's mouth but turns his stomach sour. The opportunity to speak

God's Word is always sweet, though the words may be bitter. Such will always be the case with those called upon to bring God's Word to the world, as they continue to prophesy about peoples, nations, tongues, and kings.

5. The Two Witnesses (11:1–14)

The world's response to those who prophesy in God's name is shown in the account of the two witnesses. John is called upon to measure the temple of God and the altar and to count the worshipers. While the events which follow take place, the true church rests under God's protection. The outer court, however, has been handed over to the Gentiles, in this case those who claim to be people of God but in reality are not.

The "holy city" will be trampled upon for 42 months, that is, three and a half years, that symbol of the time of Satan's attacks against the church, namely the entire age of the church; and the two witnesses will prophesy among the unrighteous for that same period of time, now called 1,260 days, but will not be killed until their testimony is complete, that is, until all have heard the Gospel.

Rather than seeing these two witnesses as specific individuals who will come to the world when the time of the end is near, the witnesses should be understood as the Word of God itself, which will be proclaimed in the world as long as the world lasts. Nevertheless, the descrip-

The
World Shaken,
God's Kingdom
Stands Firm

Revelation 8:1–11:19

STUDY

4

Resources for Worship

Use these resources for your daily study. They may be used again during the week's assembly.

Hymn

If God Himself be for me,
   I may a host defy;
For when I pray, before me
   My foes, confounded, fly.
If Christ, my head and master,
   Befriend me from above,
What foe or what disaster
   Can drive me from His love?

I build on this foundation,
   That Jesus and His blood
Alone are my salvation,
   The true, eternal good.
Without Him all that pleases
   Will vain and empty prove.
The gifts I have from Jesus
   Alone are worth my love.

No angel and no gladness,
   No high place, pomp, or show,
No love, no hate, no badness,
   No sadness, pain, or woe,
No scheming, no contrivance,
   No subtle thing or great
Shall draw me from Your guidance
   Nor from You separate.

For joy my heart is ringing;
   All sorrow disappears;
And full of mirth and singing,
   It wipes away all tears.
The sun that cheers my spirit
   Is Jesus Christ, my king;
The heav'n I shall inherit
   Makes me rejoice and sing.

(*Lutheran Worship* 407:1–2, 5–6)

Prayer

O blessed Holy Spirit, You are the omniscient guide and omnipotent guardian of the Christian church in this world of sin and confusion. Without You we would be misled and lost. We see the world shaken and disturbed, yet Your kingdom stands firm. Continue to protect and guide us through Your Word that we may steadfastly follow Your guidance and safely arrive at the place prepared for us, as our home forever. We make our request boldly in the name of Christ, the Lord! Amen.

Digging Deep
My Personal Study
for Week 4   *Revelation 8:1–11:19*

In Revelation John reports seeing a series of visions. The vision reported in chapters 5 through 7 reveals events that will occur from Christ's ascension to His return at the end of time. These events have been heralded by the opening of seven seals. Chapter 8 begins with the opening of the seventh seal, which introduces the next vision, which will feature the sounding of seven trumpets. This vision also will reveal what will take place between Christ's ascension to His return in glory—but from a different perspective. This vision will emphasize that these events are initiated and controlled by God Himself.

Day 1   Read Revelation 8:1–13

1. This opening of the seventh seal inaugurates the next vision. After a period of impressive, expectant silence, seven angels appear and are issued seven trumpets. But before the trumpets are sounded, another angel appears with a golden censer, a firepan on which were burning coals for the burning of incense. Incense was to be offered twice a day in the Old Testament sanctuary (Exodus 30:7–8). In John's vision, what accompanies the smoke of the incense as it rises before God (v. 4; see also Psalm 141:2)?

2. **Challenge Question.** The angel hurls the censer to the earth and thunder, rumbling, lightning, and an earthquake result—as when God came down upon Mount Sinai (Exodus 19:16–19). What does the hurling of the censer of incense to the earth represent (Exodus 3:7–8a)?

3. The first four trumpet blasts bring calamities upon the earth (remember that four is the symbolic number referring to the earth). Compare these calamities with events that occurred when God sent Moses to bring God's judgment upon the Egyptians:

a. Verse 7 and Exodus 9:22–26.

b. Verses 8–9 and Exodus 7:20–21.

c. Verse 12 and Exodus 10:21–23.

d. The main purpose of making these comparisons is not to say that there will be a *literal* repetition of the plagues upon Egypt but to learn of God's ongoing actions (throughout the ages) toward His people and their oppressors. What can we learn from Psalm 78:51–53 and 2 Peter 2:9?

4. At the trumpet blast by the third angel, a star given the name Wormwood (a plant with a bitter taste) falls from the sky and turns water bitter. Read Exodus 15:23–25a. What do these two events—opposite from one another—suggest about God's judgment and grace?

5. Note that the calamities resulting from the sounding of the first four trumpets are visited upon the world of nature and that the devastation is partial ("a third"). How does this reflect what Jesus predicts in Matthew 24:4–7?

Day 2   Read Revelation 9:1–21

As bad as were the calamities brought about by the sounding of the first four trumpets, they were nothing compared to the calamities now to be introduced. These trumpets will produce woes (8:13).

6. The sounding of the fifth trumpet results in the opening of the Abyss. Read Matthew 8:12; 13:42; Luke 8:26–31; and 1 Peter 3:19. What "unpleasant" features of the Abyss are suggested by these texts?

7. a. Notice that the creatures (described as locusts) from the Abyss may not harm those who are marked with God's seal, that is, those in whom the Holy Spirit dwells. Read Revelation 9:11. The leader of this locust-like horde of tormentors is called the angel of the Abyss and is identified by Hebrew and Greek words, both meaning Destroyer. Why is this an appropriate name for this leader (1 Peter 5:8)?

b. *For personal meditation.* Think about God's promise, here, to shield you from the devil's power, and His call to you to "resist him [the devil], standing firm in the faith" (1 Peter 5:9). In the privacy of your heart, confess to God your Father now any incident in your life when you gave in to the devil's wiles. Then claim His forgiveness for the sake of Jesus, letting His Word of forgiveness and power sink in as you thoughtfully read Romans 8:26–39.

8. The sixth trumpet releases an army of mounted troops. Compare the effect of this army to the horde released by the fifth trumpet. (Compare 9:5–6 and 9:15, 18.)

Our Victorious Lord Leads through Trouble to Triumph

Revelation 4:1–7:17

God Himself is in control of all of history, and Christ, the Lamb of God, has earned the right to reveal the future to us. He does not tell us everything we would like to know. However, he *does* tell us all we need to know to be assured that Christ has already triumphed over the evil powers at work in the world, and that His people will be preserved from all spiritual harm even in the midst of the worst catastrophes that will come upon the world.

1. A Glimpse of Heaven (4:1–11)

The vision begins as John is invited to look through an open door into the throne room of heaven. The center of this vision is the throne. The one on the throne is none other than God Himself. He is described in terms of the glow of precious stones—the green of jasper and the red of carnelian. His throne is surrounded by a rainbow, which serves as a sign of His covenant with His people. The seven lamps are the seven spirits, that is, the Holy Spirit, who is coequal in majesty with the Father and the Son.

Surrounding the throne are the 24 elders. They represent the church in its totality. They also are seated on thrones and they wear crowns, showing that they live and reign with God Himself, as Christ promised would be the case with His people (cf. 20:4). They are dressed in white, having been clothed in the

righteousness of the Lamb. The sea of glass shows God's holiness and his Lordship over all things. The mysterious "four living creatures" represent all creation—the wild and domesticated animals of the land, the birds of the air, and humanity. The six wings call to mind the seraphim (Isaiah 6:2), and the faces are those of the "living creatures" of Ezekiel 1, who in Ezekiel 10 are called "cherubim." Their task is to serve God, first of all through their singing and adoration, which they do continually. To this song the elders, and so all of God's people, respond by laying their crowns before God, declaring that all they have and are comes from God Himself. This glimpse into heaven provides the backdrop for the rest of the book. The God who created the heavens and earth rules over His creation. He alone is worthy of honor, and, in the end, He alone will receive it.

2. The Scroll and the Lamb (5:1–14)

From the glorious panorama of the throne room of God, John's attention is now called to the scroll which God holds in His right hand. The scroll tells "what must soon take place" (1:1; 4:1); that is, it holds the future. Opening the scroll will not only tell what must take place; it will also bring it about. It is locked with seven seals, completely sealed so that no one can divine the future. Yet the future is in God's hand. No human being,

indeed no creature, has the right to open the seal and see what is to come; nor can any mere creature bring it about. The cry of the angel, "Who is worthy to break the seals and open the scroll?" (v. 2) is met with silence. No one is worthy—except one! As the elder announces, the Lion of Judah (Genesis 49:9–10), the Root of David (Isaiah 11:1), who is the Lamb of God, is worthy to open the seals. By His triumph the Lamb has won a victory which enables Him to show the future to the people of God—a future which will bring about in time the victory already won for eternity.

The image of Jesus as Lamb, though rare elsewhere in the New Testament, is permeated with Old Testament imagery. The lamb was a sacrificial animal whose blood was shed in sacrifices for atonement. Most significant was the Passover lamb, whose blood was shed and marked the doorposts of God's people in Egypt and thus preserved them from death. These sacrificial lambs foreshadowed the death of the Lamb of God, the shedding of whose blood was a sacrifice that needed to be made only once for the sins of the whole world. God in His wisdom, and to further show His control of history, let His Son be put to death on the day of Passover. But the Lamb who was slain now stands before the throne of God, risen and victorious.

Here we see the Lamb's spiritual

attributes set forth in physical language. He stands in the center of the throne, that is, at the seat of God Himself. He now has been given back all the honor which He forsook for our sake. He is described in terms of seven, the number of completeness—seven horns (all-powerful) and seven eyes (all-seeing), which are the seven spirits.

Since Christ's ascension the sevenfold Spirit has been sent out into all the world to proclaim the victory the Lamb has won. Thus the victorious Lamb, the one who had been slain, takes the scroll from the right hand of God and prepares to open the seven seals. Then the honor and glory that in chapter 4 were given to the one on the throne are given in turn to the Lamb. All of the beings around the throne join in the song and are accompanied by the prayers of the saints (5:8).

3. The Opening of the Seals (6:1–17)

Though the victorious Lamb is the one who opens the seals, it is not triumph, but rather calamity, which is first revealed. The opening of the first four seals releases in sequence the infamous "four horsemen of the apocalypse," whose coming is announced each in turn by the four living creatures. The first horseman is a conqueror, riding a white horse, the symbol of purity and of victory. While his description is similar to that of Christ in 19:15, he is but an imitation, allowed for a time to set himself up as a ruler of this world—hence, an Antichrist, that most blatant symbol of human pride, who seeks to be

honored as God. Christ Himself warned of the coming of false Christs (Matthew 24:4–5).

The second horseman, riding a red horse, brings bloodshed to the world with his sword, as he takes peace from the world and causes men to turn against one another in warfare. Again, this should be no surprise, as Christ declared that in the last days there would be "wars and rumors of wars" (Matthew 24:6).

The third horseman, riding a black horse, is famine, which follows in the wake of warfare. He carries a pair of scales, indicating the care with which the precious remaining food is doled out among the people.

The fourth horseman, riding a pale horse, is death, followed by Hades. How can such calamities as conquest, bloodshed, and famine end, except in death?

The four horsemen are given power over "a fourth of the earth," that is, they do not reign over the whole world, but only a portion, albeit a significant portion.

With the opening of the fifth seal, the scene moves from earth to heaven. Here we see the "souls under the altar," that is, those whose lives have been poured out like sacrificial blood because of their faith. These saints have already received the white robe which is the righteousness of Christ, and there are more to come. God delays His justice so that His mercy can be displayed on even more people. Though the wait seems long, God will not bring things to an end until the

number of those who would be put to death as they had been is completed. But, He assures them, they will be vindicated. In the midst of the horrors of this world, God remains in control.

Then, with the opening of the sixth seal, God begins His final judgment. The very foundations of the universe will be shaken— the earth with the earthquake, and the sky as sun and moon are darkened and the stars fall from the sky. Then the sky recedes "like a scroll" (Isaiah 34:4), as God rends the heavens and comes down (cf. Isaiah 64:1). Then the people of this world— there are seven classes listed, signifying completeness—turn and run as they seek to hide themselves from God. The wrath of God is so terrible that even being covered by the mountains would be preferable to facing it. When that day of wrath comes, no one can stand.

4. The People of God on Earth and in Heaven (7:1–17)

The picture then shifts from those who stand under the wrath of God to the people of God. The powers of destruction are not unleashed until the servants of God are sealed by God. These are 144,000 in number: 12 x 12 x 10 x 10 x 10. The number of the church squared times the cube of 10, signifying completeness. These represent the entire Christian church on earth. Note that these verses do not indicate that the people of God will be removed from the world before the end. While they are not preserved *from* the suffering the world endures because of sin, they are preserved *in the midst* of it, and

| Our Victorious Lord Leads through Trouble to Triumph

Revelation 4:1–7:17 | STUDY
3 |

Resources for Worship

Use these resources for your daily study. They may be used again during the week's assembly.

Hymn

The Church's one foundation
  Is Jesus Christ, her Lord;
She is His new creation
  By water and the Word.
From heav'n He came and sought her
  To be His holy bride;
With His own blood He bought her,
  And for her life He died.

Elect from ev'ry nation,
  Yet one o'er all the earth;
Her charter of salvation:
  One Lord, one faith, one birth.
One holy name she blesses,
  Partakes one holy food,
And to one hope she presses
  With ev'ry grace endued.

Through toil and tribulation
  And tumult of her war
She waits the consummation
  Of peace forevermore
Till with the vision glorious
  Her longing eyes are blest,
And the great Church victorious
  Shall be the Church at rest.

Yet she on earth has union
  With God, the Three in One,
And mystic sweet communion
  With those whose rest is won.
O blessed heav'nly chorus!
  Lord, save us by Your grace
That we, like saints before us,
  May see You face to face.

(*Lutheran Worship* 289)

Prayer

Lord God, heavenly Father, we offer before You our common supplications for the well-being of Your church throughout the world, that it may be so guided and governed by Your good Spirit that all who profess themselves Christians may be led in the way of truth and hold the faith in unity of spirit, in the bond of peace, and in righteousness of life! Send down upon all ministers of the Gospel and upon the congregations committed to their care the healthful spirit of Your grace, and that they may truly please You. Pour upon them the continual dew of Your blessing in the name of Jesus Christ, the Savior of the world and the Head of the church. Amen. (*LW* p. 128)

Digging Deep
My Personal Study
for Week 3   *Revelation 4:1–7:17*

Day 1   Read Revelation 4:1–11

1. The scene shifts from the church amidst sin and sorrow on earth to the serene majesty of God on His throne in heaven. What do the following features of this scene tell you about God?
a. The throne. (Revelation 4:2; Psalm 47:8)

b. God's appearance. Jasper and carnelian are precious stones, reflecting light with a flashing brilliance. (Revelation 4:3a; 1 Timothy 6:16)

c. The rainbow. (Revelation 4:3b; Genesis 9:12–17)

d. The 24 elders on the 24 thrones. Remember that 12 is the number of the church—12 tribes in the Old Testament, 12 apostles in the New Testament. (Revelation 4:4; Matthew 19:28)

e. The sea of glass, which may refer to the large basin outside the Old Testament temple, which was called the Sea. Priests used this basin to cleanse themselves before serving in the temple, Exodus 30:17–21; 1 Kings 7:23–25. (Revelation 4:6; Ephesians 5:23–27.)

f. The four living creatures. (Revelation 4:6b–8; Psalm 50:10–11)

Note: The seven lamps are explained as representing the sevenfold Spirit or seven spirits, that is: the Holy Spirit. Remember that seven is the number of completeness.

2. a. Why would this heavenly scene be so helpful or encouraging to the church at the time of John? (Think about the circumstances of the seven churches in chapters 2 and 3.)

b. What is helpful or encouraging about this scene to you, as a Christian and part of the church today?

3. What is the major theme of the heavenly songs in verses 8 and 11?

Day 2   Read Revelation 5:1–14

The vision continues, focusing on two objects, first a scroll, then a Lamb. The two objects are connected.

4. a. The scroll is in the right hand of God, who is seated on His throne. What is the significance of God's right hand (Exodus 15:6)?

b. The scroll symbolizes the future in which God would carry forward and consummate His plan of salvation. Significantly, the scroll is completely sealed (note, *seven* seals), so that no one can open it or see its contents. Why would the terms "Lion of the tribe of Judah" and "Root of David" give courage and hope to the weeping John (Genesis 49:8–10; Matthew 1:2,17; Isaiah 11:1; Romans 15:12)?

5. a. Read Revelation 5:6. Summarize some of the meaning of "Lamb" that is "slain" (Exodus 12:21–23; Isaiah 53:6,7; John 1:29; 1 Peter 1:18,19).

b. Notice that in Revelation 5:8–14 all creation (the four living creatures) and the church of both the Old Testament and the New Testament (the 24 elders) worship Jesus (the Lamb). (The sevenfold Spirit, or seven spirits, refer to the Holy Spirit, who is closely associated with the work of Jesus by spreading the Gospel into all the world.) Read the songs that are sung in verses 9–10, 12, and 13b. Write a brief paragraph that expresses your own praise to Jesus.

The Triumphant Christ Speaks to His Church

John, an apostle of Jesus Christ, was in exile on the island of Patmos in the Aegean Sea because of his testimony for Jesus. (See figure 3 in review leaflet 1.) Rather than deny his Lord and submit to the emperor's command to honor him as a god, rather than cease preaching the Gospel of the Lord whom he knew and loved, John was willing to go into exile. That he identifies his situation with that of other believers is clear, as he identifies himself as his readers' "companion in the suffering and kingdom and patient endurance" (Revelation 1:9).

Christ Himself appeared to John, inaugurating a series of visions by which Christ would comfort His church. The Lord begins to tell him "what must soon take place" (Revelation 1:1). This first set of visions is specifically addressed to seven congregations in Asia Minor. In every case there is an exhortation to remain faithful and the promise that Christ will always be with His people.

1. The Appearance of the Triumphant Christ (1:9–20)

This is a spiritual portrayal using physical imagery. God, who has revealed Himself in Jesus Christ, is the God of all ages. He is the one "like a son of man," who is referred to in Daniel 7:13, the one who comes with the clouds of heaven. He wears a robe down to His feet,

the style worn by the high priest of the Israelite religion (Exodus 28:4; 29:5). The golden sash indicates that He occupies the office of high priest. His hair is white like wool, the symbol of wisdom and purity.

In Daniel 7 it is the "Ancient of Days" whose hair is "white like wool," so we see a clear connection between the Son and the Father. What belongs to the "Ancient of Days" likewise belongs to the Son of Man. His eyes are like blazing fire, indicating penetrating insight: all that human beings seek to keep hidden nevertheless is laid open to the eyes of Christ. His voice has the "roar of rushing waters," a description given to the voice of God in Ezekiel 43:2.

As Jesus Himself states (1:20), the seven stars in His right hand represent the messengers ("angels") of the churches, most likely the pastors of the churches, and the seven lampstands among which He stands represent the seven churches to whom the seven letters which follow are being sent, and by extension the whole church on earth. Like a lampstand, the church does not produce the light of the world, but it rather bears the Light of the world, Christ Himself, by speaking the Word of God which has been committed to it.

Isaiah 49:2 tells us that the mouth of the servant of God will be made "like a sharpened

sword." The New Testament says that the Word of God is the "sword of the Spirit" (Ephesians 6:17), and is "sharper than any double-edged sword" (Hebrews 4:12). So the image of the sword coming out of Christ's mouth is quite appropriate. Our Lord governs the world by no other way than by His Word.

The Christ who appears to John by His very appearance shows Himself to be victorious. His face shines like the sun. When John, quite understandably, falls at the feet of Christ, he hears the words "Do not be afraid," words heard many times before by the people of God who have witnessed God's mighty acts.

The events to come show Satan's last-ditch attempts to destroy the work of Christ, to turn the world away from Him, but in the resurrection of Christ it is made clear to us that the victory has already been won. Jesus has the keys to death and Hades, has released His people from their power and will ultimately condemn the wicked to eternal destruction.

2. The Letters to the Churches (2:1–3:22)

A map of Asia Minor will show the cities mentioned to be in a horseshoe pattern, from Ephesus at the southwestern tip to Laodicea at the southeastern tip. (See figure 3 in review leaflet 1.) These cities all lay on a major thoroughfare, making it possible

for the letters to them to be widely disseminated. As major centers of Asia Minor, the worship of the emperor would be especially strong in those cities, and the threat of persecution especially strong. There is no doubt that the problems mentioned were literal problems being experienced by those congregations. Nevertheless, since the number 7 itself indicates completeness, the seven churches, though real congregations, represent the entire Christian church of all times and places.

The letters to the seven churches generally follow the same format: (1) the greeting; (2) a title of the risen Christ based on the description in chapter 1; (3) a word of praise, beginning "I know"; (4) a criticism; (5) a warning; (6) an exhortation, beginning "He who has an ear"; and (7) a promise, which will reach fulfillment in the closing chapters of the book (Revelation 20–22). Some of the churches are doing well, some have problems brewing, and yet others are in grave spiritual danger. Faith brings victory because it clings to the one who has already emerged victorious.

A. Ephesus (2:1–7)

Ephesus, greatest city in Asia Minor at that time, was the center for worship of the goddess Artemis (Diana). (See figures 1 and 2.) Her temple was one of the seven wonders of the ancient world. Paul had a successful ministry there, and the congregation was well established through his preaching. Christ here praises the congregation for its hard work and its perseverance in the faith—how it refused to tolerate the wicked and tested those who claimed to be apostles but were not. They are also praised for hating the practices of the Nicolaitans (2:6), a sect which sought to compromise with pagan society, proclaiming that Christian liberty allowed them to practice idolatry and immorality, thus allowing them to avoid suffering for the faith.

However, while the Ephesians were commended for their zeal, they are also called upon to repent. The Ephesians were doing what was outwardly correct, but their hearts were not right, and they were again in danger of falling under God's judgment. Christ calls them to continual self-examination and repentance lest they be lost.

B. Smyrna (2:8–11)

To the church at Smyrna, a powerful and beautiful city in which Greek and Roman culture flourished, Christ has nothing but praise and encouragement. Already being persecuted by the Jewish population, they are warned to be prepared for further persecution. Nevertheless, they are told not to be afraid, because by being faithful they will inherit a crown of life (2:10).

C. Pergamum (2:12–17)

Pergamum, the northernmost of the seven cities, was the administrative center of the province, and emperor worship was strictly enforced there. It thus is the "city where Satan lives" (2:13). Jesus is pleased that the church was remaining faithful even though Christians were being put to death there. However, they are also warned against tolerating those who "hold to the teachings of Balaam" (2:14) and of the Nicolaitans (2:15). When Balaam was unable to curse Israel, he counseled Balak to entice Israel into immorality, thus bringing a curse upon themselves. So both groups would tempt the church to compromise with the surrounding culture and bring about the downfall of many in the church.

To those who continue the fight, Christ promises His heavenly food, that is, eternal life. They will also receive a "white stone with a new name" (2:17), which serves as their admission ticket to the heavenly banquet. The "new name" signifies the beginning of new life for those who turn from their old way of life to Christ.

D. Thyatira (2:18–29)

The Christians at Thyatira are praised for growing in love, faith, service, and perseverance. Nevertheless, they were guilty of tolerating "Jezebel." The name is a code name for a false prophetess active in the city, given the name of the wife of Ahab, King of Israel, who had actively sought to destroy the worship of the true God and replace it with the worship of Baal. Perhaps the attitude of love being conveyed by the people became misguided and led to tolerance of an evil that should have been cast out from among God's people. The exalted Christ warns these Christians that they are being enticed into both idolatry and adultery. "Jezebel's" coming

The Triumphant Christ Speaks to His Church

Revelation 1:9–3:22

STUDY 2

Resources for Worship

Use these resources for your daily study and at the week's assembly.

Hymn

O Jesus, King most wonderful!
　O Conqueror renowned!
O Source of peace ineffable,
　In whom all joys are found:

When once You visit darkened hearts,
　Then truth begins to shine,
Then earthly vanity departs,
　Then kindles love divine.

O Jesus, light of all below,
　The fount of life and fire,
Surpassing all the joys we know,
　All that we can desire:

May ev'ry heart confess Your name,
　Forever You adore,
And, seeking You, itself inflame
　To seek You more and more!

Oh, may our tongues forever bless,
　May we love You alone
And ever in our lives express
　The image of Your own!

(*Lutheran Worship* 274)

Reflection

Perhaps you have heard or read this statement: "Whenever God erects a house of prayer, the devil builds a chapel right next door." The truth of that becomes very real to us, as God's people, when we look at the seven churches to whom the triumphant Christ writes a letter in the book of Revelation. "He who has an ear, let him hear what the Spirit says to the churches" (Rev. 2:7, 11, 17, 29; 3:6, 13, 22).

Prayer

O Christ Jesus, our triumphant ever-present Lord of the church, You told Your disciples and all of us, "Where two or three come together in My name, there am I with them" (Matthew 18:20). Keep us conscious of this in all our Christian fellowship in prayer and Bible study and ministry. We delight in Your presence and rely on Your support in all our activity. In Your holy name we pray. Amen.

Digging Deep
My Personal Study
for Week 2   *Revelation 1:9–3:22*

Day 1   Read Revelation 1:9–20

1. a. How does John describe himself and his circumstances in verses 9–10?

b. What does John imply about the circumstances of his readers in these same verses?

2. a. Note the way Christ is described in Rev. 1:7–8 and 12–18. Compare this passage to Daniel 7:13–14. What do both of these passages tell us about Jesus?

b. Which feature of Christ in verses 12–16 do you find most impressive?

3. a. Within this description of Jesus' glorious majesty (vv. 12–20), we find a reference to the Gospel—the Good News of our salvation through Christ. Find and record this Gospel statement.

b. What does this Gospel statement mean to you personally?

4. Notice that John sees Jesus standing *among* the seven golden lampstands (v. 13). In verse 20 John identifies the seven lampstands as the seven churches mentioned in verse 11. The seven stars are identified as the angels, or messengers, of the seven churches (most likely referring to the pastors). In chapter 2 Jesus addresses a message to each of the angels of the churches. What encouragement to churches do you find in these references to the lampstands and the stars (vv. 12–13, 16, 20)? (See also Matthew 18:20.)

Day 2   Read Revelation 2:1–29

5. Which of the churches in the second chapter can be identified as follows?
a. Tempted to compromise

b. Encouraged to be faithful

c. Left its first love

d. A temptress in its midst

6. Paul had ministered in Ephesus perhaps 40 years previously (Acts 19:1–41), and this church became one of the most prominent congregations in the first centuries of Christian history.
a. For what does Jesus commend this church (Revelation 2:1–3)?

b. For what does Jesus fault this church (vv. 4–6)?

7. Compare the messages to the churches in Pergamum (vv. 12–17) and in Thyatira (vv. 18–29).
a. What two problems faced both of these churches?

b. In what way do you think it might be said that churches today are called upon to deal with these same problems?

The book of Revelation holds great fascination for Christians and has done so ever since it was written. The real purpose of the book is to give comfort to Christians at all times. When God's people fear that the world is raging out of control, they see here that God is always in control of history.

1. Apocalyptic Literature

Revelation is written in a style which is quite different from the other books of the New Testament, a style known as "Apocalyptic." Apocalyptic writing occurs in the books of Ezekiel, Daniel, and Zechariah in the Old Testament. Since apocalyptic writings had been used to bring great comfort during times of trouble and persecution, Jewish readers particularly would have recognized the book of Revelation for what it is—a book of encouragement in time of trouble, when the temptation to fall away from the faith or to compromise the faith would have been very great.

Apocalyptic literature takes the form of visions, and these visions transcend the events of history. The visions go above and beyond the present and take into account the whole of history, from the beginning to the end, and show that God is in control of history. In fact, in Revelation God describes Himself as "the Alpha and the Omega" (Revelation 1:8), using the first and last letters of the

Greek alphabet to show that everything from beginning to end is under His control.

The imagery in the visions and the use of symbolic numbers serve both to uncover (the term "Apocalypse," the Greek title of the book of Revelation, means "uncovering") and to cover. It uncovers the truth to those who are privy to the "code book" needed to decode the writing, while it keeps the truth hidden from the outsider. In Revelation, and in apocalyptic literature in general, history is seen as a spiritual battleground in which the forces of good and evil contend for final control of the earth and its inhabitants.

2. Interpreting Revelation

Scholars have offered four different methods of interpreting the book of Revelation, each based on different assumptions as to the purpose and message of the book. (See figure 1.) The "preterist" view sees the events of the book happening entirely in the past, specifically at the time of John. The "futurist" view sees the entire book, except for the first three chapters, as lying in the future, the events not taking place until immediately before the return of Christ. The "idealist" view sees the book speaking symbolically of such timeless truths as the victory of good over evil. The "historical" view sees Revelation presenting in symbolic manner the entire history of the church from the time of Christ up to the last

judgment and into eternity. In this understanding, the seven visions in Revelation each cover the same period of time—the entire age of the church—each vision describing the same events from a different perspective and adding a little more to what was presented in the earlier visions. This last understanding is to be preferred because it uses proper methods of interpreting the Scriptures.

3. Historical Background

The John who wrote this book was undoubtedly also the John who wrote the gospel account and the three letters which bear his name. The vision we have recorded in this book (the title is Revelation, in the singular) was given to him while he was in exile on the island of Patmos, a small rocky island off the coast of Asia Minor (see figure 3), where he had been sent for refusing to compromise his faith. The time is about the year A.D. 95. By this time John was quite old, and, tradition tells us, was living in the city of Ephesus, in the Roman province of Asia.

By the time Revelation was written, Caesar worship was the most widespread and most widely practiced religion of the Roman Empire. Domitian, who ruled the Roman Empire from A.D. 81 to 96, bestowed divine honors upon himself and his predecessors, and gave himself the title "Lord and God." He required that once a year all residents of the empire appear

before a magistrate and burn a pinch of incense to the emperor as god. If they met this one requirement, they would be allowed to worship any other god or goddess of their own choosing.

How tempting it must have been to offer that one small sacrifice to Caesar, and then to be let alone to worship according to one's own conscience! The opening letters to the congregations in Asia and indeed the whole of the book of Revelation come out of the call to remain faithful even in the face of death.

4. Certainty for an Uncertain Future (1:1–3)

The opening sentence notes that God gave this revelation to John in order to show what "must soon take place." God desires to give certainty in the midst of an uncertain future, but only on His terms. God's people will be blessed when they take this book to heart, because "the time is near." The time of persecution has arrived for God's people, and the words of this book provide them with the strength to endure by pointing them to the final victory.

The revelation given to John that comprises the content of this book is given through God's "angel." Whenever angels speak, the message is to be heard as though coming from the mouth of God Himself. Angels are active in carrying out God's judgment against the world throughout Revelation and also are active in the war against the armies of Satan. We see the war between God and Satan waged

on two stages—the spiritual stage and the earthly stage. This revelation comes to John in the midst of this spiritual battle, as the forces of Satan, using the government of the Roman Empire, sought to destroy the church of God, through forcing either apostasy or death. Through apocalyptic imagery, Christians are promised that they already have the victory, even though that victory is visible only through the eyes of faith. This message of hope is conveyed in a way which only Christians can understand, since only Christians have the knowledge which unlocks the code to the apocalyptic message.

5. The Old Testament Key (1:4–8)

Already in these opening verses it becomes clear that the "code book" which unlocks the Revelation to John is nothing other than the Old Testament. As we enter into a study of Revelation, we will see many strange creatures and awesome events, but many of them are referred to in the Old Testament as well. When you recognize the "coded" nature of the book of Revelation you can begin to make sense of the various numbers that occur in the book. The numbers in Revelation are important for understanding the message of the book. The meanings of the numbers remain consistent throughout, and knowing the proper meaning will enable you to see the message. (See figure 2.)

The first significant number to appear in Revelation is the number 7. The number 7 is the

most common number used in the book and is the number of completeness, perfection, or holiness. Seven in turn is the sum of two other numbers standing for completeness: 3, which is the number of God (the Triune God, Father, Son, and Holy Spirit), and 4, the number of the world (the four directions of the compass). The number 3 ½, a half of 7, is always associated with the evil forces which oppress the church, usually those spiritual and religious in nature. This number comes in several variants as well: "a time, and times, and half a time," in chapter 12; 42 months or 1260 days (3 ½ years) in chapters 11 and 12. The number 12 refers to Old Testament Israel (the 12 tribes) and New Testament Israel, the church (the 12 apostles). Ten and its cube, 1,000, represent completeness. These may be multiplied and combined to get important illustrative combinations: 24 (Old Testament plus New Testament churches); or 144,000 (12 x 12 x 1000 represents the whole people of God, past, present, and future).

As we move through the book, we will see how these numbers illustrate God's truth to us, how they tell us what must soon take place, and how they are given to us to comfort us in the midst of our struggles in life. May that declaration of hope and of certain victory be uppermost in your minds!

Resources for Worship

Use these resources for your daily study and at the week's assembly.

Hymn

Jerusalem, O city fair and high,
  Your tow'rs I yearn to see;
My longing heart to you would gladly fly,
  It will not stay with me.
Elijah's chariot take me
  Above the lower skies,
To heaven's bliss awake me,
  Released from earthly ties.

O happy day, O yet far happier hour,
  When will you come at last,
When by my gracious Father's love and pow'r
  I see that portal vast?
From heaven's shining regions
  To greet me gladly come
Your blessed angel legions
  To bid me welcome home.

The patriarchs' and prophets' noble train,
  With all Christ's foll'wers true,
Who washed their robes and cleansed sin's
      guilty stain,
  Sing praises ever new!
I see them shine forever,
  Resplendent as the sun,
In light diminished never,
  Their glorious freedom won.

Unnumbered choirs before the shining throne
  Their joyful anthems raise
Til heaven's arches echo with the tone
  Of that great hymn of praise.
And all its host rejoices,
  And all its blessed throng
Unite their myriad voices
  In one eternal song.

(*Lutheran Worship* 306)

Reflection

Very appropriately Pastor Johann Meyfart of Coburg, Germany, wrote this hymn, "Jerusalem, O City Fair and High," as the conclusion of his sermon in 1626 on the theme: "On the Joy and Glory Which All the Elect Are to Expect in the Life Everlasting," Matthew 17:1–9. It is a hymn coming out of the Thirty Years' War, yet it is fitting for today.

Prayer

Lord Jesus, our victorious Savior, we recognize that we must endure many hardships to enter the kingdom of God. Send Your Holy Spirit through the means of grace to keep us steadfast in triumphant faith as we travel through this world of sin and sorrow, until we are safe forever with You in heaven, for Your mercy's sake. Amen.

Digging Deep
My Personal Study
for Week 1   *Revelation 1:1–8*

Day 1   Read Revelation 1:1–2

1. What do the opening verses of Revelation tell us about the message of the book and its transmission?

2. The word "apocalyptic" comes from a Greek word that means "to disclose." Revelation is the only apocalyptic book in the New Testament. "Apocalyptic" refers to writings that are rich in references to "the last days" and in symbols of angels and animals and numbers. List apocalyptic features in the texts below. Do not attempt to interpret the verses at this time.
a. Revelation 4:7–11

b. Revelation 8:2–6

c. Revelation 13:18

d. Revelation 19:17–21

e. Revelation 20:2–3

3. What does 2 Timothy 3:16–17 tell us about the origin and purpose of the apocalyptic writings we find in the Bible?

Day 2   Read Revelation 1:3

4. a. In apocalyptic writing, as here in Revelation, two kinds of angels are pictured, good and evil. In the first verse a good angel brings a message that results in blessing for those who read, hear, and keep the message which the angel brought to John. What blessing is brought by an angel in Revelation 14:6?

b. What does Revelation 12:7–9 tell us about the origin of the evil angels?

c. Who is the leader of the evil angels (Revelation 12:9)?

d. What assignment has God given to the good angels concerning you (Hebrews 1:14)?

e. Why should angels not be worshiped (Revelation 19:10)?

Day 3   Read Revelation 1:4–5a

5. The book of Revelation is written in the form of a letter with John, the apostle whom Jesus loved, as the writer, 1:1, and the seven churches of Asia Minor (Turkey today) as the addressees, 1:4, 11. Name the cities in which these seven churches were located.

6. Which verse or verses in Revelation 1:1–8 tell us that:
a. Jesus Christ is both the receiver and the giver of revelation?

b. Revelation is an eyewitness account by John?

c. Both the reader and the hearer will gain a blessing?

d. The fulfillment of promised future events is imminent?

e. What Jesus did, He did for our salvation?

7. John uses a literary device, known as "triads" (three related terms grouped together) a number of times in these verses, e.g. in 1:4: "from Him who is, and who was, and who is to come." (Also in verse 4 all three persons of the Holy Trinity are mentioned. "Him who is, and who was, and who is to come" refers to the Father; the "seven spirits" refers to the Holy Spirit, the perfect and complete Spirit; Jesus is mentioned directly.) Find other triads in the first five verses of chapter 1.

Day 4   Read Revelation 1:5b–6

8. Revelation presents an entirely new attitude toward Christians on the part of the government of the Roman Empire. Previously there was a form of

religious liberty (Acts 16:36–40; Acts 22:30). But now conditions were changed. The current Roman Emperor, Domitian (A.D. 81–96), demanded that he be worshiped as a god (Caesar worship) and confronted Christians with the absolute choice of worshiping Caesar or Christ. The punishment for defying this demand was death.

a. Put yourself in the place of a Christian at this time, and meditate on each of the terms that describe Christ in verses 5–8. Which of these terms do you think would be most meaningful for John and the other Christians suffering persecution?

b. From the descriptions of Christ that you found in part a. of this question, try to make your own word-portrait of Christ.

Day 5   Read Revelation 1:7–8

9. Two other features of the book of Revelation require attention and explanation to help us in our Bible study: the use of numbers and of Old Testament allusions and references. Some of the more commonly used numbers are: seven (7); three (3); three and one-half (3 ½); four (4); twelve (12); and one thousand (1,000). Precise interpretations are not always possible, but here are some general interpretations: Seven (7) is the number of completeness, holiness, and perfection, based on the seven days God used to complete His creation

(Genesis 1). Three (3) is next to seven in indicating completeness (three persons in the one triune God). Three and one-half (3 ½) refers to periods of particularly harsh persecution. Four (4) refers to a completed square and may symbolize mankind (4=humans plus 3=God, totals 7 = God in perfect relation to humans). Twelve (12) reminds us of the 12 tribes in the Old Testament and the 12 apostles in the New. So 12 (and multiples of 12) suggests the church. One thousand (1,000) represents large numbers with definite boundaries set by God. Practice applying these interpretations to the numbers in the following verses:

a. 1:4—The seven churches represent:

b. 4:4—The 24 elders sitting on 24 thrones represent:

c. 7:4—The 144,000 (12 multiplied by 12 multiplied by 1,000) represent:

d. 20:3—The 1,000 years during which Satan remains locked up represent:

e. 21:12, 14, 21—The heavenly city (with features in twelves) represents:

10. In regard to Old Testament allusions, it is interesting to note that Bible scholars have found 348 references in 278 of the 404 verses that comprise the book of Revelation, but not one direct quotation mentions an Old Testament writer specifically. What reference is made to the Old Testament in each of the following passages? (Do not try to interpret the passages at this time.)

a. 2:14 (Numbers 24:25)

b. 2:20 (1 Kings 16:31)

c. 5:5 (Genesis 49:8–10)

d. 7:5–8 (Genesis 49)

11. What do these frequent allusions to the Old Testament suggest to you about the unity of Scripture and about the importance of Old Testament study today?

12. Which verses of Revelation 1:1–8 are most meaningful to you, and why?

LifeLight™ © 1993 CPH   20-2317

Figure 1.   Methods of Interpreting Revelation.

Method	Characteristics
Preterist	Refers only to events in the time of John.
Futurist	Refers only to events that take place immediately before the return of Christ.
Idealist	Timeless truths, such as the victory of good over evil.
Historical	Symbolically presents history of church from ascension of Christ to last judgment. Seven visions describe same events from different perspectives.

Figure 2.   Symbolic Meaning of Numbers in Revelation.

Number	Symbolic Meaning
3	God
4	earth
7	completeness, perfection, holiness
3 ½	evil forces that oppose church; limited time given to the devil to persecute the church
10	completeness, entirety
12	church

Note: Multiples of these numbers heighten or expand their meaning.

Figure 3.   The Seven Churches of Revelation.

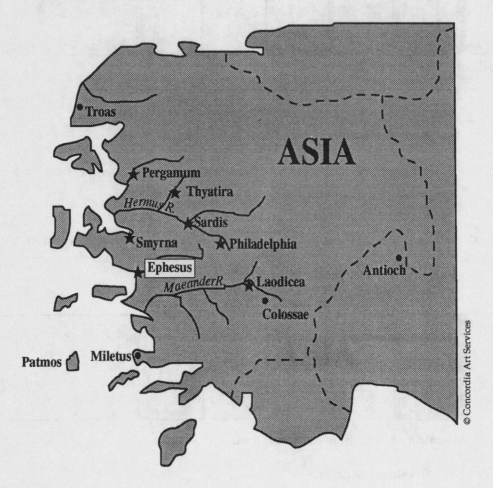

Figure 4.   Outline of This Course.

Session 1	Understanding the Book of Revelation (1:1–8)
Session 2	The Triumphant Christ Speaks to His Church (1:9–3:22)
Session 3	Our Victorious Lord Leads through Trouble to Triumph (4:1–7:17)
Session 4	The World Shaken, God's Kingdom Stands Firm (8:1–11:19)
Session 5	Christ's Victory over Satan and His Hosts (12:1–14:20)
Session 6	Praise for God and Armageddon for the World (15:1–16:21)
Session 7	The Agony of the Wicked and the Ecstasy of the Saved (17:1–19:21)
Session 8	The Millennium and the Doom of Satan (20:1–15)
Session 9	Our Victorious Lord Reigns Forever (21:1–22:21)

Day 3   Continue Revelation 2:1–29

8. Which church, in your opinion, was the strongest and which the weakest of the four in this chapter? Give reasons for your choice.

9. Revelation 2:10b is a favorite passage for many people. What specific problems faced the church in Smyrna (vv. 8–10)?

10. Jesus identifies Himself as He "who has the sharp, double-edged sword" (v. 12). Refer back to 1:16. Considering that this sword comes out of Jesus' mouth, what do you think is meant by this sword? (Refer also to Hebrews 4:12.)

11. Jesus refers to Himself in verse 18 as "the Son of God, whose eyes are like blazing fire and whose feet are like burnished bronze."
a. The blazing eyes see both the strengths (v. 19) and the failings of this church (v. 20). How does God's penetrating sight into every corner of your life encourage you?

b. The feet "like burnished bronze" are able to crush all opposition to Jesus and His kingdom. How does this characteristic of Jesus encourage you?

Day 4   Read Revelation 3:1–22

12. Read verses 1–3. Put in your own words the fault that Jesus found with the church in Sardis.

13. Read verses 7–13. Jesus is said to hold the key of David, which opens and shuts the entrance into God's kingdom. That key is the Gospel, through which we receive (and share with other repentant sinners) the forgiveness of sins. (See Matthew 16:19, where Jesus declares He will operate these keys through the church.) What assurance does the fact that the key to God's kingdom belongs to Jesus give to us (Revelation 3:8)?

14. a. For what does Jesus rebuke the church in Laodicea (vv. 14–18)?

b. What counsel does Jesus offer to this church and to Christians today who have the same problem (vv. 19–20)?

Day 5   Review of Revelation 1:9–3:22

15. Review the messages to all of the churches mentioned in chapters 2 and 3. Remember that seven is the number of completeness—suggesting that these seven churches are meant to represent a composite of Christian churches of all time. Make a list of those qualities for which Jesus commends and rebukes the churches.

Church	Commends	Rebukes
a. Ephesus (2:1–7)		
b. Smyrna (2:8–11)		
c. Pergamum (2:12–17)		
d. Thyatira (2:18–29)		
e. Sardis (3:1–6)		
f. Philadelphia (3:7–13)		
g. Laodicea (3:14–22)		

16. Consider the situation of Christianity in our own part of the world today. Go back to question 15 and underline those qualities (both positive and negative) that you think apply to us Christians today.

17. **Challenge Question.** Find the attribute or descriptive reference to the triumphant Christ that is mentioned at the beginning of each letter to the seven churches. How does each attribute fit the needs of each of the churches? (To help you get started, the answer to the first part of the question is provided.)

a. The church in Ephesus (2:1–7): Jesus holds the seven stars in His right hand and walks among the lampstands. He will hold them with His power (His right hand) as they resist false apostles. But, if they do not return to their first love, He will remove their lampstand from its place (remove them from their position of leadership among the churches).

b. The church in Smyrna (2:8–11)

c. The church in Pergamum (2:12–17)

d. The church in Thyatira (2:18–29)

e. The church in Sardis (3:1–6)

f. The church in Philadelphia (3:7–13)

g. The church in Laodicea (3:14–22)

18. What most vivid insight have you gained from these letters regarding the relationship of the triumphant Christ to the Christian church today?

destruction is announced, and those who tolerated her behavior are called upon to repent. Genuine love will not tolerate evil, but will condemn it.

E. Sardis (3:1–6)

The problem in Sardis was spiritual lethargy. Christ declares that, though they had a reputation for being alive, they are in fact dead. He urges them to wake up. It may be that, since there were no major problems in the church at Sardis there was nothing to challenge them— nothing to keep them sharp— and as a result they had sunk into a stupor. They looked fine outwardly, but in fact were only going through the motions of the faith. There were still some in Sardis who were "worthy," that is, who still had faith and so were truly active in service for their Lord. To those, he gives the promise that they will be "dressed in white," clothed in the righteousness of Christ.

F. Philadelphia (3:7–13)

Jesus has nothing but praise for the church in Philadelphia. Though the people of the church are perceived as having little strength, they have nevertheless remained faithful. They were being attacked by Jews who refused to acknowledge Jesus as Messiah, but are assured that at the judgment these people will be forced to acknowledge that Christ has loved them. They are encouraged to remain faithful and are promised that they will be preserved from the hour of trial. They are promised that they will be inscribed with the new name given by Christ Himself.

G. Laodicea (3:14–22)

The church at Laodicea is in the worst condition of all. They are "lukewarm"; they have no zeal for the Lord at all. Though outwardly rich, they were spiritually wretched. Christ warns them that if they do not change He will spit them out of His mouth (3:16). But He has not yet abandoned them. He pleads with them to repent so that they will be restored and will live and rule with Christ.

God's people still need to take those warnings to heart, for the temptations of that time remain temptations today. But the promise of victory which has already been won by Christ still is ours today as well.

Figure 1. Ruins of Ephesus. These ruins of the theater of Ephesus are among all that remain of Ephesus today. From this theater a beautiful marble street with colonnades led to the harbor, one-third mile away.

Copyright © Paul Maier. Used by permission.

Figure 2. A statue of Diana (Artemis) found in an excavation of old Ephesus. Ostrich eggs, symbols of fertility, decorate her dress above the waist. Below the collar are signs of the zodiac.

Copyright © Paul Maier. Used by permission.

Figure 3. Road from Pergamum to Asclepion. Pergamum is on the hill in the distance.

Copyright © Paul Maier. Used by permission.

8. The sixth calamity (vv. 12–17) comes upon the entire world, without exception. What calamity is this (Mark 13:24–27)?

9. Read Matthew 24:33–44. Why is God telling you what to expect in this period before Christ comes again?

Day 3   Read Revelation 6:1–17

As the Lamb opens the first six seals one by one, a series of six calamities come upon the earth. The opening of the seals represents the disclosure of what is going to happen on the earth until the end of this age, when Jesus returns.

6. The first four seals release four horsemen, each riding a horse of a different color. Carefully read what is said about each horseman to determine what calamities each horse and rider represent. These calamities affect the whole world.
a. The white horse and its rider (v. 2; Matthew 24:4–5).

b. The red horse and its rider (vv. 3–4; Luke 21:9).

c. The black horse and its rider (vv. 5–6; Luke 21:11).

d. The pale horse and its rider (vv. 7–8; Ezekiel 5:12).

7. The fifth coming event (vv. 9–11) is a calamity that affects the church specifically. What calamity is this (Matthew 24:9)?

Day 4   Read Revelation 7:1–8

Those who ignored and despised God's warning about judgment to come will experience "the wrath of the Lamb." The last verse of Revelation 6 says: "The great day of their wrath has come, and who can stand" before it (6:17)? What about the believers and the church? God gives us the answer for believers still on the earth 7:1–8 and believers who are already in heaven in 7:9–17.

10. Before "the great day of wrath" (6:17) is allowed to come, "the servants of our God" are sealed.
a. Read Exodus 12:1–7; 12–13. How were the Israelites sealed to protect them when the Lord passed through Egypt to strike down the firstborn?

b. God gave Abraham circumcision as a seal. What did this seal of circumcision represent (Romans 4:11a)?

c. What seal has God given to Christians (Ephesians 1:13–14; 4:30)?

11. In Revelation 7:4–8 the number who receive the protective seal are 144,000—12,000 from each of 12 tribes of Israel. The 12 tribes here represent believers.
a. Remembering that 10 and its multiples is the number of completeness, what does the 144,000 represent? (The 144,000 is the result of $12 \times 12 \times 10 \times 10 \times 10$.)

b. What comfort does this offer to you? (As you consider this question, read John 10:27–30.)

Day 5   Read Revelation 7:9–17

As much reason as there is for songs of praise in the church on earth, so much more there will be songs of praise in the church in heaven.

12. What does verse 9 tell us about who will be in heaven? (Note that *four* groups are mentioned. What significance does this number have here?)

13. Compare verses 9b and 13–14. What do the white robes and the palm branches represent?

14. What chief (most important) doctrine in the entire Bible is underscored by the cry of the saints in heaven (vv. 10, 12)?

15. Read verses 15–17 slowly and thoughtfully. Which phrases in these verses mean the most to you? (Be prepared to tell your discussion group why you chose the phrases you did.)

16. Review the first seven chapters of Revelation. List several truths you have learned from these chapters that you think can inspire Christians to live in this world with an attitude of confident hope and gratitude.

they are preserved by nothing other than the Word of God.

At verse 8 the scene shifts again, moving from the church on earth to the church in heaven. Here the people of God are described as "a great multitude that no one could count, from every nation, tribe, people, and language," the same four groups mentioned in 5:9, though in different order. The multitude stands clothed in the righteousness of Christ and stands before the throne, as did the heavenly chorus in chapter 4. Here, finally, the triumph won through the death of the Lamb is finally realized in all of its fullness. What God has promised has been brought to pass. Preserved through their trials, they will live and serve God for eternity. Their eternal state is described in terms of the miseries of this world which they will no longer experience.

So, the scene ends in heaven, where it all began. These things "must" take place, in order that God's justice may be meted out and His people vindicated. The terrors of this life are real and they are disturbing, but the people of God can look at them and see the hand of God behind them.

Figure 1. The Temple during Christ's Earthly Ministry. Refer to this drawing while using study leaflet 4, questions 14 and 20. Note the Holy of Holies, which contained the ark of the covenant, concealed by a curtain; also the balustrade that kept Gentiles from entering the temple proper.

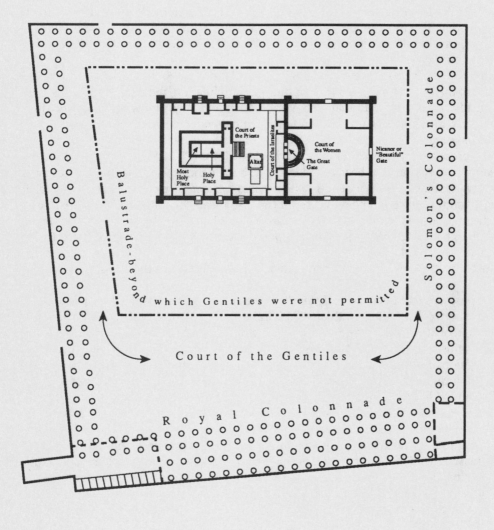

© Concordia Art Services

Figure 2.   What Scripture Says about Hell. Read this article as preparation for study leaflet 4.

HELL (ETERNAL PUNISHMENT)

1. The doctrine of eternal punishment, repugnant to natural man, has been repudiated by errorists (e.g., Origen, Universalists) but is clearly revealed in Scripture. To deny this doctrine is to reject the authority of Scripture.

2. According to the Bible, the unbelievers will be damned (Mk 16:16). They will be punished with everlasting destruction (2 Th 1:9), the damnation of hell (Mt 23:33). This punishment is variously described as unquenchable fire (Mk 9:43–48), outer darkness, where there will be weeping and gnashing of teeth (Mt 8:12), a prison from which there is no escape (Mt 5:25–26).

3. As regards the question whether the fire of hell (Mt 25:41 et al.) is a material fire or not, restraint is in order. Since other expressions are used to depict the suffering of the lost (e.g., "their worm does not die," Mk 9:48; they "shall be cast out into outer darkness," Mt 8:12), all of them may well be understood figuratively. The description that the Bible gives of hell is to express in terms taken from human experience the unspeakable torments of body and soul of the damned. Whatever has been said about the awful doom of the wicked is intended to call sinners to repentance and warn them of the wrath to come.

4. As the essence of heaven is fellowship with God, so the essence of hell is exclusion from this fellowship. Deprived of the blissful presence of God and the glory bestowed on the believers (2 Th 1:9; Mt 25:41), the unbelievers will languish in the company of the evil spirits to bemoan, in abject despair, their willful impenitence during the time of grace and their unalterable condemnation (Mt 8:12). This punishment, which is never alleviated, will be eternal in the two-fold sense that it suffers no interruption (Lk 16:24–26) and has no end (Mk 9:48). Degrees of punishment are clearly taught (Mt 11:22–24; Lk 12:47–48). Those who spurned the proffered grace and knew the Lord's will, will be punished more severely than those who never heard the Gospel. Hypocrites who devour widows' houses and for a pretense make long prayer shall receive the greater damnation (Mt 23:14). Wherein this difference consists has not been revealed, and we should not presume to know.

5. To identify the destruction of the wicked with annihilation (see *Annihilationism*) has no warrant in Scripture. If the punishment of the wicked consisted in their outright annihilation, the Bible could not speak of it as *everlasting* destruction (2 Th 1:9). According to Romans 2:8–9 tribulation and anguish await those who do not obey the truth; according to John 3:36 the wrath of God abides on those who do not believe the Son. Neither could be predicated of men who cease to have a conscious existence. Destruction or perdition, when contrasted with life, denote not cessation of existence, but eternal misery, the loss of everlasting blessedness (Ph 1:28).

6. The meaning of "eternal" has been called into question on the ground that the Greek word *aionios*, translated by "eternal" or "everlasting," does not denote "endlessness." *Aionios* (from *aion*, "age") is a relative term and may mean "age-long," "enduring for a time only," but it can also mean "everlasting," "endless," and it clearly has this meaning in all passages that speak of the destiny of men in the hereafter. The *temporal* is contrasted with the *eternal* (*aionios*) (2 Co 4:18; 1 Ptr 1:23–25). When judgment is pronounced, the wicked will go into *everlasting* punishment, but the righteous into life *eternal* (Mt 25:46). The same Greek word is used in both sentences. If *aionios* denotes endlessness in the one, it must have the same meaning in the other. The punishment of the wicked is unending misery and woe (Mk 3:29).

7. The same passages that unequivocally teach the eternity of punishment rule out as unscriptural the teaching of the ultimate salvation of all men. 1 Corinthians 15:22, Ephesians 1:10, and Revelation 21:5 cannot be adduced as proof for the final salvation of all, for when the Scriptures speak of the ultimate goal of the world's history, they refer only to the blessed perfection of the faithful. 1 Corinthians 15:28 and related passages teach the final victory of the kingdom of God, the subjugation of all the enemies of Christ; they do not state that all these enemies will be converted to God.

8. No physical location of hell is intended by what Scripture says of the habitation of the wicked. Hell is where God reveals Himself in His vindictive justice to the finally impenitent.

9. One of the objections raised to the doctrine of eternal punishment is that it is inconsistent with the love of God to condemn men to unending perdition. But it must be remembered that while God is a God of love, His love is only one of His attributes. Justice is also one of His attributes. Since God is a perfect being, we find in Him the perfect and harmonious expression of all His attributes. It is significant, too, that the most solemn and explicit declarations of eternal punishment recorded in Scripture were spoken by the forgiving and compassionate Savior (Mt 25:41, 46; Mk 9:43–48). Some hold that it is unworthy of a just God to punish men with everlasting condemnation. But how can man presume to determine the justice of the infinite God according to human conceptions of justice? (Ps 19:9; Is. 55:9; Ro 11:33).

From *Lutheran Cyclopedia*, revised edition. (St. Louis: Concordia, 1975), pp. 373-74.

LifeLight™ © 1993 CPH   20-2312

9. For what purpose (though not successfully realized) were the vicious hordes released by the fifth and sixth trumpets (vv. 20–21)?

Day 3   Read Revelation 10:1-11

Once more future events have reached the point where God's judgment is about to come upon all humankind. A mighty angel appears to announce this judgment, but he is put off for a time.

10. Identify the angel described in 10:1 and what this verse means to tell us through the imagery of the rainbow (Genesis 9:8–17), the cloud and fiery pillars (Exodus 13:17–18,21–22), and face like the sun (Matthew 17:1–2).

11. The angel stands on sea and land (showing that all creation is subject to God the Judge) and shouts a lion-like roar in which are heard seven thunders. The thunders represent God's judgment, and that there are seven thunders tells us that this is God's complete and final judgment. But before the judgment can be pronounced, it is postponed by a voice from heaven. What does Peter tell us about the seeming delay of God's judgment in 2 Peter 3:8–9?

12. John is directed to eat the little scroll (Revelation 10:9). What does this action signify (v. 11)?

13. a. The little scroll tastes as sweet as honey. Note what Psalm 119:103 says about God's Word. What about God's Word makes it sweet to you?

b. *For personal meditation. Sharing optional.* Afterward, however, the little scroll becomes sour in John's stomach. Read Ezekiel 2:8–3:8. Like Ezekiel, who went "in bitterness and in the anger of my spirit, with the strong hand of the Lord upon me," we too may be called to speak God's Word of Law and judgment upon persistent evildoers. We speak God's Word of Law in all its severity in order to call people to repentance, so that we may then also share the sweet message of His forgiving love. What message of Law would God have you speak to someone who needs to be called to repentance (a son or daughter? a co-worker? a friend?)? Ask for His Spirit to give you the courage to speak—in blunt honesty and in love.

Day 4   Read Revelation 11:1–14

The vision continues to show what will happen before the final judgment. We are now told of measuring the temple of God and of two witnesses (who will be discussed in question 17).

14. John is told to measure the temple and to count the worshipers within it. The measurement of the temple, like the seal placed upon the people of God in the earlier vision (7:3–4), is to set limits to protect God's people from harm. The outer court of the temple, however, is not measured. (See figure 1 in review leaflet 3.) "Gentiles" (those who are not God's people) appear to be within the church but are not (Revelation 2:9). These false believers will abuse the church (God's temple) for 42 months, or three and a half years. As seven is the number of completeness, three and a half represents the limited period during which Satan wields his power on this earth. During this limited period of time (1,260 days is the same period of time as 42 months or three and a half years) when false believers trouble the church, two witnesses prophesy (speak God's Word).

a. They are called olive trees and lampstands. Read Zechariah 4:1–6, 11–14. Compare Revelation 11:3 and Zechariah 4:6. How does God empower the witnesses?

b. The two witnesses wear sackcloth, a coarse, dark cloth that symbolizes repentance and sorrow for sin. In what ways were these witnesses similar to John the Baptist (Matthew 3:4)?

c. When the two witnesses are attacked, fire comes out of their mouths and devours their opponents. What do you think is represented by the fire that comes from their mouths (2 Kings 1:10; 2 Thessalonians 1:7–9)?

15. The beast from the Abyss (the devil from hell) is allowed to attack the two witnesses and kill them, which causes great rejoicing on earth. But after a short time (three and a half days), God raises them and takes them up to heaven in a cloud while their enemies look on. When will this take place (1 Thessalonians 4:16–17; Revelation 1:7)?

16. Who are these two witnesses? Perhaps they represent Moses and Elijah, preeminent prophets who were opposed by unbelievers and who appeared with Jesus when He was transfigured, or appeared in His glory, before His disciples Peter, James, and John (Matthew 17:1–3). But, in a broader sense, they represent the prophetic voice of the church which testifies about Jesus until the end of this age, despite the opposition of the devil and the unbelieving world. What's frightening—and what's encouraging—to YOU as you witness to your faith and participate in the Great Commission (Matthew 28:20)?

Day 5   Read Revelation 11:15-19

These verses complete the third vision (Revelation 8–11), which featured the sounding of the seven trumpets. As with the second vision (Revelation 4–7), which featured the opening of the seven seals, this vision concludes with the judgment and God's victory over His enemies. (The first vision featured the seven letters to the churches, Revelation 1–3.)

17. Loud voices in heaven declare that "our Lord and . . . His Christ" begin an eternal reign over "the kingdom of the world" (v. 15). With what event will the reign of Christ be made evident to all (Matthew 24:30–31)?

18. For what event—and why—do the 24 elders give thanks in verses 16–18 (Romans 14:9–12)?

19. Compare Psalm 2:1–12 with the songs of praise and gratitude of God's people in this vision. In that light, give your own paraphrase of: "The kingdom of the world has become the kingdom of our Lord and of His Christ and He will reign for ever and ever," Revelation 11:15, as your statement of trust amidst life's problems as a disciple and witness of Christ.

20. The final event of this vision occurs when God's temple is opened so that the ark of the covenant can be seen. In the Old Testament temple the ark was placed within the innermost room, the Most Holy Place, where only the high priest might enter—and he only once a year, on the day when he made atonement for the sins of God's people. What do you think is signified by the opening of the temple, so that the ark of the covenant is in full view? (Consider Matthew 27:50,51; Hebrews 10:19–22 as you answer this question.)

Figure 1.	The First Four Trumpets and the Ten Plagues.	
1.	Hail and fire, mixed with blood. A third of the earth, a third of the trees, and a third of the green grass are burned up.	Plague of blood. Waters of Egypt turn to blood.
2.	Mountain thrown into the sea. A third of the sea turns to blood, a third of sea creatures die, and a third of the ships are destroyed.	Plague of frogs. Frogs cover the land.
3.	Star (named Wormwood) falls to earth. A third of the waters turn bitter, and many people die. (Does not recall one of the plagues but the sweetening of the waters of Marah [Exodus 15:22–26]).	Plague of gnats. Dust of the earth becomes gnats.
4.	A third of the sun, a third of the moon, and a third of the stars turn dark. A third of the day and a third of the night is without light.	Plague of flies. Dense swarms of flies throughout the land.
		Plague on livestock. Egyptian livestock dies.
		Plague of boils. Painful boils break out on people and animals.
		Plague of hail. Hails strikes people, animals, and vegetation in Egypt.
		Plague of locusts. Locusts devour everything left by the hail.
		Plague of darkness. Egypt turned totally dark for three days.
		Plague on the firstborn. Firstborn males of Egyptians and their cattle die.

tion of these two witnesses calls to mind Moses, who stood alone among the Egyptians, who called down plagues upon the nation until God's people were freed, and Elijah, who dried up the skies to express God's judgment against King Ahab of Israel (1 Kings 17:1) and who called down fire from heaven at Mount Carmel (1 Kings 18:16–45).

After three and a half days of revelry, in which the citizens of this supposedly great city show their disgust for the witnesses by allowing their bodies to remain in the street, they are brought back to life by the breath of God. Their work completed, they are taken up into heaven, as Moses was after his death, as Elijah was without dying. They are taken up in a cloud as was the Lord Himself after His resurrection. Once again the divine hand behind these events is seen in the occurrence of an earthquake. Those who survive the earthquake give glory to God.

6. The Seventh Trumpet (11:15–19)

With the completion of the second woe, the seventh trumpet is sounded. At the sound of the final trumpet, "The kingdom of the world has become the kingdom of our Lord and of His Christ." The time of trial for the people of God is past; the time of judgment for the enemies of God has come. The judgment is again revealed from heaven with the revealing of the ark of the covenant, the sign of God's presence with His people from the wanderings in the wilderness to the end of the monarchy.

Nevertheless, God's Word continues to be proclaimed in the world, driving people to repentance and comforting them with the knowledge that through Christ they are in God's hands. The Word of God stands firm in the midst of the instability of the world, and God keeps His people safe, even as the world rejects them and the message they proclaim.

Figure 2. Identification of the Four Kingdoms. Refer to this chart as you complete study leaflet 5.

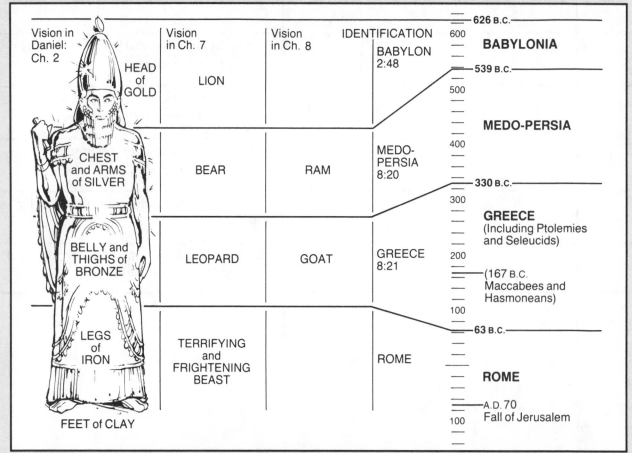

Taken from THE NIV STUDY BIBLE. Copyright © 1985 by THE ZONDERVAN CORPORATION. Used by permission.

Day 3   Read Revelation 13:11–18

Now John sees a second beast. This beast serves the first beast, and both beasts serve the dragon (Satan).

10. Notice that the second beast has something of the appearance of a lamb but speaks like a dragon, reminding us of Jesus' warning in Matthew 7:15. What examples are there from your everyday life or from the culture around us of a dragon (wolf) in lamb's clothing?

11. Three times (13:3, 12, 14) we are told that the first beast had been wounded and yet lived. Read 2 Thessalonians 2:9. In what way might the fatal wound that had been healed be a counterfeit sign to mislead the unwary? Consider also Matthew 24:24.

12. Read verses 14–15. The second beast performs great and miraculous signs to deceive the inhabitants of the earth and lead them to worship the beast. What seemingly "miraculous signs" do we see today in false religions and cults, and in technology wonders we may be tempted to rely on instead of God?

13. Besides the use of deceiving signs the second beast uses another method to obtain the loyalty of people, the threat of death and withholding the necessities of life (vv. 15–17). Give examples of that in recent history and in current affairs.

14. Much speculation has been given to the number of the beast, 666 (v. 18). John identifies it as "man's number." Remember that seven is the number of completeness or perfection; six would fall short of perfection. Despite the beast's deceptive appearance ("horns like a lamb," v. 11) and ability to do "great and miraculous signs" (vv. 13–14), the beast is not God or of God but is of Satan. How do you obtain the wisdom (v. 18a) that will keep you from being deceived by Satan and his agents? Read and think about 1 Corinthians 2:6–16 before you answer.

So who or what does the second beast represent? Take note of the purpose of his activity; it is to promote the purposes of Satan. This beast represents all teaching, propaganda, and efforts throughout history to undermine the doctrine of Christ and to advance the work of the devil.

Day 4   Read Revelation 14:1–13

Meanwhile, back in heaven . . . . The scene now shifts briefly to heaven. In contrast to the earth, where many are deceived by the dragon and the two beasts, the saints in glory worship the Lamb and follow Him wherever He goes. Then, the scene shifts again to the earth, but this time we focus not on the dragon and the beasts but on three angels, each with a message to proclaim.

15. What is meant by Mount Zion (v. 1)? See Hebrews 12:22–24.

16. *For personal meditation. Sharing optional.* The 144,000 (as in Revelation 7:4–8) represents the complete number of the saints (believers) in heaven. This large number is the result of 12 (the number of the church) multiplied by 12 multiplied by 1000 (10, the number of completeness, times 10 times 10). They have the Father's name written on their foreheads. This indicates that they belong to God (as the mark of the beast in 13:17 indicates those who belong to Satan). Meditate, now, on the wonder of having God's name placed upon you in your Baptism (Matthew 28:19) or at some other time when you came to faith by the working of God's Spirit through the Word. Bathe in the glory of knowing you're GOD'S OWN CHILD as you slowly read Romans 8:15–17. Then speak, in your own words, as a child to your Father, thanking Him for making you a child and heir—and letting Him know any wants and needs on your heart.

17. The saints in heaven sing a new song (v. 3). Review the songs in 5:9–10, 12, 13b. What is the theme of the songs that are sung in heaven?

18. Now the scene shifts again to the earth, where three angels fly in mid-air, each with a message to proclaim. State in your own words the message of each angel:
a. The first angel (v. 7).

b. The second angel (v. 8)—"Babylon," the name of the city that fought against God's people in the Old Testament, represents Rome, which promoted idolatry and persecuted Christians, and all other institutions today that do the same.

c. The third angel (vv. 9–11)—Review your answers to the questions for Day 3 as you answer this question.

19. This day's reading concludes with a blessing (v. 13). What do the deeds of believers testify about them (James 2:18b)?

Day 5   Read Revelation 14:14–20

The vision concludes as the two previous visions have ended—with the glorious return of Christ to begin the final judgment and the beginning of the new, eternal age.

20. Read the concluding part of Jesus' parable of the weeds (Matthew 13:28–30) and its explanation (Matthew 13:40–43). What similarities to today's reading do you find in the passages in Matthew?

21. Consider the duties performed by the various figures in today's reading. Notice that the first figure with a sickle is described as like a son of man. Refer back to Revelation 1:13, 18. Notice also that this figure wears a crown of gold, a symbol of victory. Who performs the special duty to reap the righteous?

22. After the first harvest comes another harvest (vv. 17–20). What happens to those who are gathered in this second harvest (v. 19)?

23. The winepress of God's wrath is outside the city (v. 20). What city is meant (Revelation 21:2)?

24. *For personal meditation. Sharing optional.* Read Revelation 14:20. The blood flowing out of the press covers a distance of 1,600 stadia (about 180 miles). This number represents four (the number of the earth) multiplied by itself multiplied by 10 (the number of completeness) by 10 the finality of judgment upon all the earth. The blood flowing out of the winepress of God's wrath represents punishment for sin exacted upon unbelievers. Slowly read Revelation 1:5 and Hebrews 9:11–15 and think about our precious Savior shedding His blood as He suffered God's wrath in your place. In Jesus, your sin is judged, condemned, and atoned for. Then breathe a word of thanks to Jesus, who loved you so terribly much—even unto death—and who lives and loves you still!

third angel speaks to those who listen to the message of Babylon, proclaiming the frightening, and very real, specter of eternal punishment for the wicked. It is a solemn warning that evil will be punished. It also serves as an admonition to the people of God to endure to the end and to remain faithful.

5. The Final Harvest (14:14–20)

Ultimately, the end will come. When Christ has harvested His own, the angels under Him will harvest the rest of the world, pouring them into the

"winepress of God's wrath," where the execution of God's wrath is compared to the treading of grapes. The number 1,600 is four (the number of the world) multiplied by itself and then multiplied by 10 (the number of completeness) multiplied by itself, showing the finality of God's judgment on the earth. The massive outflowing of blood shows the extent of God's judgment against the wickedness of the world.

Satan is powerful. He will do everything possible to destroy

the church, and failing that, to lure or force as many people away from Christ as possible. Yet, Satan, his power, and his propaganda will all be destroyed in the end, as will all of those who have followed them. God's people, forced to suffer and even die for their commitment to Christ, will emerge victorious, singing the eternal new song before the throne of God forever.

Figure 1.   John's Fourth Vision as Pictured by Gustave Doré (1832-83). See Revelation 12:1–12.

Figure 2. John's Fourth Vision as Pictured by Albrecht Dürer. Dürer depicts especially verses 13–16 of chapter 12.

a. How is the first plague (Revelation 16:2) like the sixth plague in Egypt (Exodus 9:10–11)?

b. How are the second and third plagues (Revelation 16:3–4) like the first plague in Egypt (Exodus 7:19–21)?

8. Note the angel's comment regarding the plague of blood in Revelation 16:5–6. Relate this comment to Paul's admonition in Romans 12:19.
a. How might the awareness that God will one day punish those who persecute His people encourage you and other Christians when treated unfairly because of faithfulness to Christ?

b. What opportunity is available now to those who are guilty of persecuting God's people, as exemplified by the apostle Paul (1 Timothy 1:13–14)?

c. *For personal reflection. Sharing optional.* Opportunity for repentance and forgiveness must take place during their life (Hebrews 9:27). Death ends the opportunity and puts every individual before God our Judge. Therefore, God, I earnestly beg you to enable me, by the power of Your Spirit, to speak Your Word of Law and Gospel to _____. Help me to speak gently and winsomely, so that the power of Your love in Christ may operate

through my weakness. Grant repentance and renewal to life through faith in Christ to _____ for Jesus' sake. Amen.

9. One of the angels has commented on the appropriateness of God's act of judgment in causing the murderers of His people to drink blood. Now the altar responds in agreement. Who might the altar represent in this case (Revelation 6:9)?

Day 4   Read Revelation 16:8–15

10. a. How *might* those afflicted with these plagues have responded to them (v. 9b)?

b. How *do* they respond to them (vv. 9a, 11, 21)?

c. God allowed Satan to afflict the Old Testament believer Job very severely. Job's wife urged her husband to curse God (Job 2:9), but Job refused and said that we must trust God enough to receive trouble as well as good from God's hand (Job 2:10). Why do you think some are able to receive trouble and still trust God while others receive the same kind of trouble with cursing and refuse to repent?

11. No Egyptian plague is like the outpouring of the fourth bowl, but Scripture often connects fire with God's judgment (e.g. 1 Corinthians 3:13; 2 Peter 3:7). The outpouring of the fifth bowl results in darkness that plunges the beast and his kingdom into darkness, just as darkness was one of the plagues upon Egypt (Exodus 10:21–23). This plague causes people to gnaw their tongues with agony, and still they will not repent but only curse God. The outpouring of the sixth bowl results in the appearance of three evil spirits that look like frogs. Though similar to the plague of frogs upon

Egypt (Exodus 8:1–6), this plague is much worse.
a. What are these evil spirits, or demons, intent on bringing about (Revelation 16:14)?

b. What to you is most significant and encouraging in Jesus' words to us about the "last days" in which we now live? (See Matthew 24:9–14.)

Day 5   Read Revelation 16:16–21

12. "Armageddon" in Hebrew means "the mountain of Megiddo." While no mountain is named Megiddo, it is the name of a town and an area southwest of the Sea of Galilee and near the Mediterranean Sea where battles were repeatedly fought in ancient times. Mount Carmel is located in this area. Scan 1 Kings 18:16–40. How was that earlier struggle between God and Baal like the final battle that is to take place between God and the evil forces of this world at the end of this age?

The first six plagues reveal what will happen in the world before the time when Christ comes again. Now the seventh plague refers to that time when Christ comes at the end of time to bring the world to the final judgment. The "great day of God Almighty" (v. 14) occurs. "It is done!" (v. 17).

13. a. What signs of God's final judgment upon the evil, anti-God forces of this world do you find in Revelation 16:17–21?

b. What is the result of this judgment by God? (The reference to Babylon in verse 19 is to Satan's kingdom and followers, Revelation 14:8.)

14. None of the judgments of the seven bowls fall upon God's people but only upon those who will not repent and believe. What encouragement is being given to you as a Christian in this vision? (See also Romans 8:1–3.)

15. What do these otherwise terrifying events tell you that is encouraging to you as a Christian (Luke 21:25–31)?

there to point out that Christ's coming is imminent, and that it has been ever since the day He ascended to the Father.

Nor does the fact that the bowls of wrath do not fall upon members of the church mean that the church is no longer on earth during that time. The most insidious danger associated with that view is the notion that there will be a second chance for people who do not believe now—that they have time to repent before the end after Christ comes back for His church. Such incorrect ideas must be rejected, for they come from taking a symbolic book and reading it in a literalistic manner, and then reading their conclusions back into the rest of the Scriptures. Rather than detailing a complex series of events the sole purpose of which is to show God's glory by their fulfillment, the book restates the simple message that Christ is with His people even to the end of the age and that the victory has already been won. God's people will be saved—this evil world will be destroyed. Praise God that it is all in His hands, and that we have eternal life assured!

Figure 1. The Seven Bowls of God's Wrath.

First Bowl. Poured on the Land. Ugly painful sores break out on those bearing the mark of the beast and worshiping him. *Corresponds to sixth plague on Egypt in the time of Moses.*

Second Bowl. Poured on the Sea. Turns seawater to blood; sea creatures die. *Corresponds to first plague on Egypt.*

Third Bowl. Poured on Rivers and Springs. Water turns to blood. *Corresponds to first plague on Egypt.*

Fourth Bowl. Poured on the Sun. Sun scorches people with intense heat. *Foretaste of punishment in hell.*

Fifth Bowl. Poured on the Throne and Kingdom of the Beast. Beast's kingdom plunged into darkness. *Corresponds to ninth plague on Egypt and is foretaste of eternal punishment in hell (outer darkness).*

Sixth Bowl. Poured on the Euphrates River. River dries up, allowing frog-like demons from mouths of beast and false prophet (second beast) to go out and gather kings of the earth (ungodly world powers) against God at Armageddon

Seventh Bowl. Poured into the Air. Lightning, thunder, and earthquakes shatter devil's kingdom, and plague of hail falls upon devil's subjects.

Figure 2. The Fall of Babylon. This woodcut by artist Gustave Doré previews next week's lesson: "Fallen! Fallen is Babylon the Great! She has become a home for demons and a haunt for every . . . detestable bird" (Revelation 18:1–2).

hear the tone of that voice—is it gently imploring, fiercely demanding, or . . . ? Give reasons for your answer.

8. Three kinds of collaborators with the seductive powers of ungodliness in this world are singled out as among those who will share in the destruction of the devil and his kingdom.
a. Who are these three classes of people (vv. 3b, 9, 11, 17b)?

b. What are some ways in which people sometimes ally themselves with the ungodly forces in this world to advance their own power and influence over others?

9. What lies in the future of those people who ally themselves with ungodliness in an attempt to get ahead in this world (vv. 14–19)?

10. *For personal meditation.* God is just and punishes sin (vv. 6–8, 20). What hope is there then for us, who are also sinners? Hear God speaking to you, in a very personal way, His assurance of forgiveness, as you meditate on 2 Corinthians 5:21 and 1 Peter 3:18a.

Day 3   Read Revelation 18:21–19:10

11. Another angel is sent to throw a large boulder into the sea. As the stone swiftly sinks into the sea and cannot be recalled, so the judgment of "Babylon" comes upon it swiftly and irreversibly. Read verses 22–23 and Jesus' references to the world's end in Luke 17:24–30. What similarities to this message do you find?

12. The judgment is spoken of in Revelation 18:21–24 as the condemnation that is to come upon the ungodly world with its seductive powers in the service of Satan. For what two sins does condemnation fall upon this ungodly world (vv. 23b–24)?

13. Revelation 19:1–10 describes heaven's response to the condemnation of the ungodly world which lures people into the devil's kingdom and makes war on God's kingdom. God alone receives the credit for the victory over evil (vv. 1–3). Some might think that following the judgment Satan and his followers will be wiped out so that they cease to exist. How does verse 3 (and Mark 9:43–48) correct this view—and what are some implications for Christians NOW of the reality of hell?

14. The church and all creation (the 24 elders and the four living creatures) worship and glorify God for His great victory.

a. How does verse 7b refer to the church? (See also 2 Corinthians 11:2.)

b. What does it mean that the fine linen, the "righteous acts of the saints" (v. 8—see also Isaiah 61:10) was "GIVEN to her to wear"?

c. To what event is the church invited—and what does that event represent (vv. 7b, 9)? (See also Luke 14:15.)

15. Describe your feelings as you reflect that God has invited you to participate in this celebration in heaven of God's victory over Satan and his evil kingdom. (In the privacy of your individual home study, speak to God about it in prayer.)

Day 4   Read Revelation 19:11–16

16. The person riding on the white horse (v. 11) is not identified by name. Identify this individual by noting the following clues:

a. Compare verse 11 with 3:14.

b. Compare verse 12 with 1:14; 2:18.

c. Compare verse 13 with John 1:1, 14.

d. Compare verse 15 with 1:16; 2:12.

e. Compare verse 16 with 1 Timothy 6:15.

17. What comfort is it to you to know that Jesus is the real ruler of the nations of this world—whether they acknowledge Him or not?

Day 5   Read Revelation 19:17–21

18. Contrast "the marriage feast of the Lamb" (Revelation 19:6–9) and "the great supper of God" for the birds (Revelation 19:17–21).

19. The beast (the ungodly powers of this world) who ruled the nations on behalf of the dragon (Satan) and the false prophet (the second beast) who led people to worship the beast's image and to receive his mark (showing they belonged to the beast) are condemned and "thrown alive into the fiery lake of burning sulfur"—a horrifying picture of hell! This vision has revealed Christ as victorious over the ungodly powers of this world, with all their seductiveness and threats. Read 1 John 2:15–17. Consider the case of Demas, mentioned in Colossians 4:14 and 2 Timothy 4:10. Why do Christians need to be warned about yielding to the seductive temptations of this world?

20. What encouragement do you find in 1 John 5:18–21 as you struggle against the pull of the ungodly world around you?

4. Final Defeat for God's Enemies (19:11–21)

The one to whom all prophecy points now makes His appearance, riding a white horse. He is Christ Himself, riding out to warfare, to bring His enemies down to defeat. He is called Faithful and True, as He was back in Revelation 3:14. He wears a robe dipped in blood, showing that He goes to battle for His people, and He is known as the Word of God.

The armies that follow Him show that He is indeed the Lord of hosts, the Lord of armies. And the armies that follow Him are not dressed for battle; they are dressed in the garments of victory, the fine linen that is the garment of the bride of the Lamb.

The sword that comes from His mouth, which will strike down His enemies, is the Word of God, in this case the judgment of the Law in all of its fury. He comes as one who will rule over the nations. Lest anyone exalt themselves too highly, the one who rides the white horse wears His name on His robe and on His thigh: *He* is King of kings and Lord of lords.

Now it is time for another supper. Those who attend the wedding supper of the Lamb are truly blessed, but those who are not part of that banquet will participate in the "great supper of God," not as guests but as the meal itself. An angel standing in the sun calls to all the birds flying in midair to the great supper, to feast on the flesh of the enemies of God. The victory of the Rider over His enemies is swift. Rather than gaining victory, they simply become carrion for the birds of prey.

But not all of Christ's enemies are defeated yet. Those kings of the earth who had gathered together in the service of the beast (the beast from the sea) in their blind arrogance believe that it is still possible to win the victory. Their defeat is swift and sure. The Antichrist and the one who served him and deluded the world through false miracles are captured and thrown into the fiery lake of burning sulfur. The rest of His enemies are killed, and their flesh again serves as carrion for the birds of prey. As this vision comes to an end, we again see Christ victorious and His enemies destroyed.

Figure 1. Ancient Babylon serves as a prototype for the spiritual Babylon described in Revelation 17–19.

ourtesy of The Oriental Institute of The University of Chicago.

Figure 2. The Last Judgment. The woodcut by artist Gustave Doré previews next week's lesson: "Then I saw a great white throne and Him who was seated on it. Earth and sky fled from His presence, . . . If anyone's name was not found written in the book of life, he was thrown into the lake of fire" (Revelation 20:11–15).

resurrection (v. 5). Unbelievers also will be raised at the second resurrection, the resurrection of the bodies of the dead at Christ's second coming. Just as there are two resurrections, but unbelievers experience only one of them, so there are two deaths, but believers experience only one of them. a. What is the first death, which all (except those who are still alive when Christ comes again) experience (Ecclesiastes 12:7; Hebrews 9:27)?

b. What is the second death (Luke 16:23–24)? (See also Revelation 20:14.)

12. Why does the second death have no power over believers (v. 6; Hebrews 2:9, 14–15)?

13. Unless Christ comes again before we die, our bodies also will die. Why do Christians not have to be afraid of this reality (Philippians 1:23; 2 Timothy 4:7–8)?

Day 4   Read Revelation 20:7–10

14. Toward the end of the thousand years, Satan is released for a brief time to wage war against God and His church before being finally smashed by Jesus. During this time severe persecution will occur, and false Christs and false prophets increase in number and power to deceive (Matthew 24:15–27). Satan will enlist the ungodly, unbelieving world in attacking the church. These allies of the Satan are represented by Gog and Magog. Gog, prince of Magog, appears in Ezekiel 38–39 as a

hostile power whom God defeats and destroys. a. Compare Revelation 20:9 with Ezekiel 38:22. In both verses, how is Gog defeated?

b. *For personal meditation. Sharing optional.* What does this tell us about how believers are delivered from their enemies? As you think about this, read Psalm 46 thoughtfully and prayerfully, applying it to your own life.

15. The devil is thrown into the lake of burning sulfur, hell, to be confined there for all eternity. He is preceded (v. 10) by the beast (the ungodly powers of this world) and the false prophet (those worldly forces that deceive unbelievers). Hell as the place where the devil, his allies, and his followers will spend eternity is real. That thought should cause us to value all the more the deliverance from hell that Christ has secured for us. Read Paul's strong affirmation in Romans 8:38–39. Then write your own strong affirmation expressing your confidence that Christ has delivered you from all that might separate you from God either in this life or in the life to come.

Day 5   Read Revelation 20:11–15

16. Satan is sent forever into the lake of burning sulfur, as his allied powers in this world have preceded him. Now comes the judgment of all humankind. When Christ comes again at the end of this age, the created world will be destroyed to be replaced by a new heaven and new earth (2 Peter 3:10,13; Hebrews 1:10–12). The judgment will take place not on earth but in heaven (Revelation 20:11). Who will stand before God to be judged (vv. 12–13; 2 Corinthians 2:10)?

17. Two categories of books are mentioned as the basis for God's judgment. One category consists of "books" (plural). The other category is the "book of life."
a. What is recorded in the "books" (vv. 12–13)?

b. What judgment might anyone expect on the basis of performance (Psalm 130:3; Isaiah 64:6)?

c. What has happened to the record of the sins committed by believers in Christ (Psalm 51:1, 9; Galatians 3:26–27)?

18. The second category is the "book of life." Unlike the first category, which includes all who have ever lived, the "book of life" includes only the names of those who belong to Christ (v. 15). *Why are the names of Christians written into the Book of Life (Ephesians 2:8–9; Philippians 4:3)?*

19. If we are saved solely by God's grace, through faith in Jesus, why is it that on the Last Day Jesus talks about the good works the "righteous" have done (Matthew 25:34–36) and why is it that Revelation 20:12 states that "the dead were judged according to what they had done"? Are our good works, then, also a reason we are saved? Carefully read Ephesians 2:8–10 and Matthew 25:31–33. Then in your own words explain what the Bible says about the relationship between God's grace and "good works."

20. Following the judgment, death and Hades (where the souls of those who have perished in their unbelief are until Judgment Day) are also pitched into the lake of burning sulfur (v. 14). What does Paul call the "last enemy" of Christians (1 Corinthians 15:26)?

involved. Our names have been written in the Book of Life since before the foundation of the world. Having foreknown His people, God has brought them to faith in His Son and kept them in that faith through great tribulation until the end, when He publicly declares them to be not guilty.

It is by faith, not by works that we are saved. Our works SHOW that we are believers. They are not the basis of our salvation. When those who do not know Christ are judged, they can only be judged as sinners, and so their evil works come forth.

For us who follow Christ, our sins have been cast into the depths of the sea (Micah 7:19). Christians need not fear this "final audit," expecting to hear all of our sins presented before the world, for these have all been wiped away by Christ. We, as all people, will be judged by our works, but by God's grace only our good works remain. We will be judged on the basis of our works in order that the world may see that our faith has made a difference in our lives.

The judgment, then, upon those who have refused to believe is that which Satan and his agents received—to be thrown into the lake of fire. This is the second death—the death of eternal separation from God, to be utterly abandoned by Him, and to stand under His wrath forever. Hell consists of both abandonment and punishment.

Even death and Hades are thrown into the lake of fire. Death entered the world because of sin. Hades is that place where

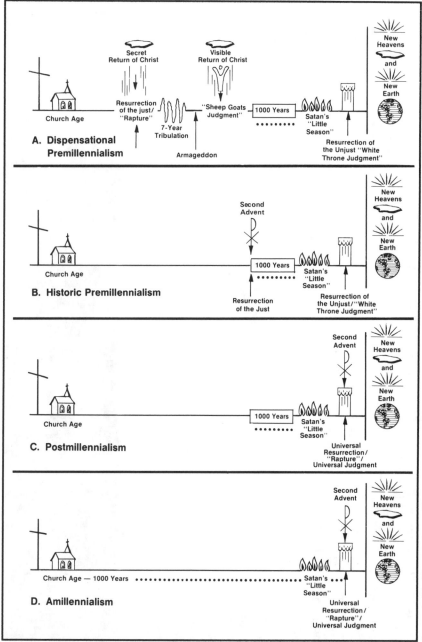

Courtesy of the Commission on Theology and Church Relations.

Figure 1. Diagrams of Millennial Views. "Premillennialism" and "postmillennialism" both teach a literal thousand-year rule of Christ upon this earth before the end of this world.

those who die apart from Christ are kept and experience the pangs of God's judgment until the time of final judgment. At the resurrection, their purpose is finished. Death has been undone and Hades has been emptied. Satan's agents, Satan himself, and all vestiges of sin, death, and Hades are cast into the lake of fire, cast from God's sight forever. Now the people of God stand before Him, ready to receive the eternal life that He has promised, for which they have been waiting so long.

Figure 2. The thousand years (millennium) described in Revelation 20 refers symbolically to the entire period between Christ's ascension and His second coming.

Satan bound; he is chained to hell so that he cannot prevent the Gospel from being proclaimed throughout the world. Satan is still active in the world, however, especially through his agents (the "beasts" of Revelation), but his activity and power are limited and held in check by God.

The thousand years (Greek: Millennium) symbolically represent the entire period of the New Testament era. A thousand is 10 (the number symbolizing completeness) times 10 times 10—the time period God has designated for this period, whose actual, literal length is known only to the Father.

The Last Day: the end of this age, the Final Judgment, and the beginning of the new age.

The Little Season and the Great Apostasy. For a brief period God will loose Satan and allow him to incite those opposed to God and His saving will to attack and seek to overcome the church. Those who have identified themselves as Christians but who do not have genuine faith in Christ will desert the church. But God will protect His people from this attack and will decisively and finally defeat and overthrow His enemies (the battle of Armageddon, a symbolic reference to God's decisive victory), including Satan himself, who will be shut up in hell forever.

11. Using John 7:37–39 as a reference, where might God the Father, God the Son, and God the Holy Spirit be referred to in Revelation 22:1?

12. No curse will be in the heavenly city (v. 3). Read Galatians 3:10–13.
a. What is the curse that hangs over people in this life?

b. How did Christ remove this curse from us—by what He did (actively) and by what He let happen to Him (passively)? (See Romans 5:19; Mark 10:45; Hebrews 2:14.)

3. Those living in the heavenly city will see God's face and will bear His name on their foreheads.
. How does seeing God's face show that all sin has been removed (Exodus 33:18–23)?

. What does having God's name on their foreheads tell us about those who live in the heavenly city (Revelation 3:12; 7:3)?

14. In the heavenly city God shares His reign with His people. Imagine what it might be like to share in God's reign. Try putting down your thoughts about what it will be like to share in God's reign.

Day 4   Read Revelation 22:6–11

15. Revelation 22:5 completes the last of the seven visions. How does a comparison of 22:6 with 1:1 show that the main purpose of the book has been completed?

16. The remaining verses, Revelation 22:6–21, are an epilogue, a closing section with a message of its own. Read verses 7, 12, 20.
a. What is the central message of the epilogue?

b. Who speaks this repeated message (vv. 13, 16)?

17. The angel instructs John not to seal up the visions he has seen (v. 10). In other words, John is to publish what he has seen and heard.
a. Since God's Word in the Scriptures has been completed and made known to the world, whose responsibility is it to believe that Word and apply it to life? (Note verse 11; see also Luke 16:27–31.)

b. What implications does this have for you as one to whom God's Word is addressed?

c. What implications does this have for you as one who addresses God's Word to others?

Day 5   Read Revelation 22:12–21

18. a. In our reading today we have Jesus' final words in the Bible. These are words that are spoken from heaven. His repeated message is that He is coming soon, a sobering and joy-inspiring thought. What is meant by "wash their robes" (v. 14)? Before you answer this question, read Revelation 7:14; Hebrews 9:14; and 1 John 1:7.

b. What does it mean to "have the right to the tree of life" and "go through the gates into the city"? (See Revelation 2:7; Genesis 3:21–24.)

19. a. What specifically does it mean that we, the bride of Christ, say, "Come" (v. 17)?

b. How are you and your church issuing this invitation?

20. Note the earnest admonition in verses 18–19. Why do you think it is so important to pass along God's Word to others conscientiously, being careful that we do not distort God's Word with our own opinions or prejudices?

21. Think about your study of Revelation. Pick one beneficial result of your study of this book and be prepared to share it with the others in your discussion group.

4. Jesus' Final Words (22:7–21)

The book is then brought to a close with words of promise directly from the mouth of Jesus: "Blessed is he who keeps the words of the prophecy in this book" (v. 7). The words are kept when we trust that God will bring about what He has promised, and when we remain faithful, if necessary even to the point of death.

John, overwhelmed with all that he had seen, falls down at the angel's feet to worship him, but the angel admonishes, "Worship God!" (v. 9). These words, coupled with the fact that John was not rebuked for falling at the feet of the exalted Lord Jesus in the same manner (Revelation 1:17), show that true worship of God includes worship of Christ as well. John is told not to seal up the words of this prophecy. On the contrary, it is to be proclaimed publicly, so that those who have ears may hear. The Word is to be proclaimed as God has set it forth, no more, and no less.

The last of the beatitudes calls to mind the host clothed in white of Revelation 7:13–14. They are the ones who are blessed because their robes have been washed in the blood of the Lamb. They have the right to eat from the tree of life. All who desire the righteousness of God, who "hunger and thirst for righteousness" (Matthew 5:6) are invited.

The invitation, "Come" (Revelation 22:17) is given by the Spirit and the bride, that is, the Spirit issues the invitation through the church. The central focus of these concluding verses is found in Jesus' declaration, "Behold, I am coming soon," a declaration made three times in the last 15 verses of the book. That declaration points first of all to the urgency of getting the message out. Second, it repeatedly assures us that the testimony in this book is true. The trials will come to an end. That which we long for so fervently is going to come to pass.

Through the visions that God granted to John, we have seen how God has been in control of history and continues to control it, bringing about His own will in the face of the world's rebellion and the stratagems of Satan and his hosts. Though the visions tell of strange, frightening, and wonderful things, the more familiar we become with the entirety of Scripture the more we become able to understand the things which will come to pass as they are recorded here. Having seen what must soon come to pass, and hearing Jesus' assurance, "Behold, I am coming soon," we, too, must respond in exactly the same way John did at the overwhelming joy of this knowledge, and say, "Amen. Come, Lord Jesus" (v. 20).

Figure 1. The Vision of the New Jerusalem as pictured by Gustave Doré. "I saw the Holy City, the new Jerusalem, coming down out of heaven from God, prepared as a bride beautifully dressed for her husband" (Revelation 21:2).